10/95

D0029646

RED BEANS

RED BEANS

POEMS BY VICTOR HERNÁNDEZ CRUZ

COFFEE HOUSE PRESS :: MINNEAPOLIS :: 1991

Some of the poetry and prose works previously appeared in *Hambone, Image Magazine, Intent, Ink, Las Americas Review, Mango Magazine,* and *Rolling Stock.* "Don Arturo: A Story of Migration" first appeared in *By Lingual Wholes,* published by Momo's Press, copyright © 1982 by Victor Hernandez Cruz. Reprinted with permission of the publisher.

This project is supported by The Bush Foundation; Dayton Hudson Foundation; Honeywell Foundation; Minnesota State Arts Board; National Endowment for the Arts, a federal agency; Northwest Area Foundation; Star Tribune/ Cowles Media Company; and James R. Thorpe Foundation.

Coffee House Press books are available to bookstores through our primary distributor, Consortium Book Sales and Distribution, 287 East Sixth St., Suite 365, St. Paul, Minnesota 55101. Our books are also available through all major library distributors and jobbers, and through most small press distributors, including Bookpeople, Bookslinger, Inland, Pacific Pipeline, and Small Press Distribution. For personal orders, catalogs, or other information, write to:
COFFEE HOUSE PRESS
27 No. Fourth St., Suite 400, Minneapolis, Minnesota 55401

Cruz, Victor Hernández, 1949-
    Red Beans : poems / by Victor Hernández Cruz.
      p. cm.
    ISBN 0-918273-91-9 : $11.95
      1. Puerto Ricans–United States–Poetry. I. Title.
PS3553.R8R44 1991
811'.54--dc20
                              91-25377
                              CIP

9 8 7 6 5 4 3 2 1

Contents

Red Beans

3 Red Means

4 The Bolero of the Red Translation

The Guayabera is the Tuxedo of the Caribbean

13 Snaps of Immigration

15 New/Aguas Buenas/Jersey

19 Agriculture

21 Trio Los Eternos

24 Al-Haram

28 Scarlet Skirt

33 Mithra

35 Christianity

36 Islam

37 Chronic Chronicles

41 Tradición

42 Corsica

44 Problems with Hurricanes

46 To El Grupo Folklórico y Experimental Nuevayorquino

48 Messages from Across the Street on Tobacco and Water Wires

51 Libros

52 An Essay on William Carlos Williams

53 Theory of Why the Night Comes

54 Versions of Basho in Spanish

55 An Evening on the River Ganges

57 Heart Surgery

59 Contradictions

60 Poesia Tropical for You

61 The Coconut Clock

63 Jíbaro Scientific Axiom

64 Weather Report

65 Igneris

68 Creole Eyes

69 Encomiendas

70 Conduits of Sound

71 Three Movements

76 Was Is

78 Areyto

82 Good Waters

84 The Troubadour's Heritage

Morning Rooster

87 Mountains in the North: Hispanic Writing in the U.S.A.

92 Celebrating Puerto Rican Style

95 Salsa as a Cultural Root

101 Foreword

102 Entreversión

104 Taos: The Poetry Bout: Codrescu vs. Cruz

108 Light-Mambo and Photography

113 The Low Writings

117 Don Arturo: A Story of Migration

122 Old San Juan

132 Some Thoughts as We Approach
    the 500th Anniversary of the Discovery of the Americas

138 The Popular Muse Belongs to Everybody

To my father
Severo Merced Cruz
Who went through it
Before I did
And now we can talk
About it

"The Prophet of Islam has said, 'Say La ilaha illa Llah and be delivered.'"

Seyyed Hossein Nasr
Knowledge & the Sacred

"Ay lo lay lah lo lay la ley lo lay lah."

Ramito
Puerto Rico's Mountain Troubadour

Red Beans

Red Means

Red be-ings
whose history is
Adam's apple
Guyaba at the
entrance
To the cave
Which Lucifer
Entered to
Terminate with
darkness
Taking that ride
up the throat
Finding the stove
of the kitchen
Where someone
Had been up earlier
Cooking Red Beans

The Bolero of the Red Translation

Migration is the story of my body, it is the condition of this age. On the island of Puerto Rico I first saw light in a wooden house a few streets from the plaza. Our early worlds become sounds, shapes, colors, voices that compose unknown syllables attached to objects that are beginning to give birth in our hands, odors that envelope from head to foot. We were like in a bowl surrounded by green mountains wherein a million mysteries resided. The town of Aguas Buenas was constantly bombarded by the creatures of the mountains, insectology of the strangest biologies and at night the sound of distant brewing, it seems that everything that had a mouth stayed up talking and yelling. The patron saint of our town a Moorish virgin, La Virgen Morena Reina de Cataluña, it was under her watchful eyes that I was baptized in that small vicinity of earth, in that Caribbean isle surrounded by water, coral reefs, a vegetación of abundant dreams of taste, crisscrossed by flowing rivers, beautiful apparitions within the saddest depressions of necessity. It was Aguas Buenas Puerto Rico 1949.

I was submitted to those airs, to those mornings full of the fragrances of café, hot bread, to palms rolling cigars, my grandfather on my mother's side was a tobacconist, as was his father before him, a trade that marched back through the societies of the indigenous Tainos since time immemorial, a plant which was known to the world of pre-Columbian America. The coquís, a unique Puerto Rican toad phenomena, printed their Morse codes upon my virgin eardrums, it was the mating whistle call of the male coquís which ranged out at night while the female slept. People came in and out of wooden doors, sometimes singing or voicing the sayings and proverbs of the age. Chickens and roosters made their lives under and above the houses, and they added their own Cucurus to the program of emitting sounds.

The great Puerto Rican migration towards New York also took my family out of that Aguas Buenas of those thens, of the early fifties, where in the tropicality of our town cement was being introduced to the earth, the streets were being paved, more and more cars were arriving like huge metallic moving houses, the distance between things was diminishing. Pictures came in from other realms, people wide-eyed jumped out of those vehicles and told stories of Rochester, of New York and the tremendous possibilities for employment. The island economy as always was a slow-moving snail. The nearby sugar cane plantation was on its last legs; the coffee growers who used to supply the markets of France and Holland spoke of hard times of strong competition from other tropical areas. Men with huge wavy pants and shoes like boats stood in clusters smoking cigarettes pointing towards the sky suggesting other dimensions.

Uniforms appeared on the bodies of the adults, the word *Korea* was everywhere, fathers and uncles left for long durations of time. The tribes began to scatter, women and children walked towards the rivers alone, the women washed clothes by banging them against the rocks. As the soldiers came back they married their sweethearts, and there was competition between plantains and babies to see who could reproduce more. People lived everywhere, even on the highest tips of mountains, on slopes where their small wooden frames defied the law of gravity. Money was as thin as air, the mountains were choked by belts, jíbaros dropped into the center of the plaza with straw hats waving like halos in the wind. Christmas music and poetry came marching in with the saints, born Christs guitared through the tongues of rum. Roving bands of musicians made assaults upon doors, dismantling into rhythm. There were troubadours between the flamboyan trees. Still, among the merry jingles and the sweetest fruits, the pressure of a changing earth rose in the form of hands that snatched people into the netherworlds. Skinny-boned cows forced their tails to wiggle to the tune of the East Trade Winds. From the alleyways and backyards I saw the world some three feet off the ground, the beings of the station jumping like frogs, prancing like headless chickens over mountains where they apparently turned to vapor.

In migration populations relieve themselves of their own heaviness, the bottom takes flight in search of juices and waters, hoping for an eventuality of peace and tranquility. Sacrifices are made for others, go under now so that those in the future could rise to the oxygen. Suitcases looked like parts of bodies, like extensions of arms and hands. These were pictures of the early morning of my life, yet they are still so fresh. The world was coming to an end, crucifixes over mosquito-netted beds, tears of the night rode down destiny's cheeks. At four in the morning at five in the morning rented cars made journeys towards the airport where people charged towards the edge of the world and jumped off.

It is on one of those waves that my own family jumped on, my father was the first to depart into the wild blue yonder, we followed some year later—myself, my mother and sister and my aunt Chela. We mounted a giant bird that was gonna take us to paradise. After eight disheveling hours we did not so much arrive to a new land as manage to shoot like in a time machine to the next age over. BANG. A world of awesome gray velocity, an air of metallic coldness, a cement much more cemented than any which we had previously observed. Another language which sounded like bla-bla-bla.

Through these migratory entanglements poetry hovered in the distance sending occasional pellets, stares into skylines and the drawings made by the flight of pigeons. The Spanish radio station was the heater, its boleros and guarachas, the trio Los Condes, the Mayaris, César Concepción, Cortijo y Su Combo, all keeping alive lyrics and rhythms that used to emanate from coastal Caribbean beaches and towns where houses, perhaps blue, perhaps pink, bowed to the bushels of guayabas. Traditions that extended into the mists of Spains and Africas, anatomy submitted to rhythm and grace, voices like sirens spraying the warm lyrics of love that now melted the snow.

2

Now things could be compared, differences spoke to each other, the negotiated worlds were put upon scales, lessons in contrast landed early. In schools Spanish was forbidden, expressiveness was curtailed. Images of industry collided with those of agriculture, but red earth remained in the mind. Not only my immediate family but all of our relatives started to show up in the new metropolis. Small towns on the island must have been evacuated as if there was a plague on the way. Consciousness galloped along the air, folding tenements into banana leafs. In my apartment there were story sessions in that grandiose manner known to all Latin Americans, el cuento campesino, phantasms arrived through coffee pots, pictures shook on walls and dead relatives peeled off. Into our living room the practitioners of espiritísmo gathered. With candles and prayers they penetrated screens in the space and contacted the voices of the dead, their hands went into whirls, their bodies danced. Catholic saints stood next to Indian heads. Africans came through the open wires, old Muhammadans hung with turbans from the ceilings. In my house the books were candles, the vapors of the wax contained parables. Paradoxes were abundant for those who could hear the language spoken by the eyes, demonstrated by the gestures. Poetry came to me and whispered, it came from its immense heaven where it has eternally kept vigil over the tongues of men. Literature I could nowhere find, it's something that comes later. The Bible, Allan Kardec's books on spiritism, foto-novelas were the first books I encountered in my environment. The rest was poetry in its sonorous state, the songs of our tradition. The poetic fulfillment is an inner manifestation, a soulful fire that spills out through mind and sound, the cheeks are jukeboxes blasting verse. Poetry falls everywhere, it is actually the most available art form. It is speech magic coming out of the gates of spontaneity, it is the ability to be still within action so as to be able to extract details which might otherwise escape back into the reality which produced them, enjoyed only by omnipresence. Bring into yourself the image of a man spinning a penny atop a needle during a hurricane. Poetics is the art of stopping the world, asking it the basic question: Where are you coming from? Putting a mirror in front of its big face, deciphering its emotional ingredients, speculating on its intent. Through poems everyday events are given meaning beyond themselves, life is elevated, physical actions are compared to invisible reasons, life which can drag in the tedious is given flavor, suggestions and possibilities open up onto our existence. A poem is the report card of our awareness, the temperature of our feelings. A poem is not just about what it is about but about all the multiples of associations that it carries with it. A poem about a pair of eyes can become the history of a civilization, a dance form can have mathematical meaning. Perception is the blood of the words, the stars have been out all day but the very light kept them from us. Air stops being ether and becomes angels. We have been breathing angels, our lungs are temples. Poetry is not a profession but a possession, our dedication to it is both willing and unwilling, it is a spiritual hobby that uses the technological systems contained within language to give flower.

It takes a while to recognize that the messages, or approaches of thoughts, have patterns, that they have a formula. They are not random formulations out of some kind of chaos. The right word seems to follow the right perception at the point of its must urgent necessity. All things in life seem to come this way, energy and ideas come like ambulances to get us out of emergencies.

Poets develop areas of concern, specialization, preoccupations which last years and parade in and out of individual poems written about different subjects and in various moods. Poems develop character, a personality as if they were human beings exposing themselves to us. The proper marriage of spirit and vocabulary make for what we can call a perfect delivery of an inner dialogue. A poetic life includes periods when there is an overabundance of either spirit or language. These scribblings contain much static and inevitably leave us in a state of blurriness. With time and experience a poet learns to tune the radio, to point the antennas in the proper direction. If this harmonious state cannot be achieved, I suggest that the poet should hang it up and spare us and him or herself much confusion, or even mental damage, disequilibrium. Language is one of the strong forces of nature, and like all natural power it can cause harm if not treated according to the laws of proportion.

As we read the work of a poet we fix upon their particular orientation, their principle theme. Some poets' work concentrates upon human love relations, historical concerns, spiritual or profane sentiments, erotic love, anthropological or political searches. It isn't that they don't write about other subjects; it's just that they tend to filter everything through their own personal centers, interests, which can be in more than one area at once, though closer study should eventually show that one concern, one overpowering interest will outshine the others.

There is a lot of complexities that go on within the creative poetic act, but these mechanisms need not show up within a finely delivered poem. Energy must be shaven, trimmed, sculptured. At its most fundamental, poetry is a sonorous description of the things of this world, be they spiritual or material manifestations. Events and objects sprinkled with flavor. Everyone uses the same words but not everyone can inject them with magic, as if we had never seen them before. It is description ingrained to a style and technique that is pursuing the organic functionings of our rhythmic thought-minds. In a line of one of Federico García Lorca's poems we find a great example of that feeling for description when he talks about a lizard:

el ligardijo es una gota de cocodrilo
(a lizard is a drop of a crocodile)

3

The poems in this book represent 21 years of my effort to bring to light, to bring to the earth, that which has brewed within me. In style, tone and typography it shows many different forms. As I myself would go through personal and landscape changes, it seems that my work followed. As people we all change and within a lifetime we can come to embrace many attitudes and ideas, we can even come to accept the exact opposite of our original beliefs. Our personalities shift and swing as if wind were flying through us. We are many people at once, and verse writing brings us into confrontation with these many persons as we sit them down and ask them the same thing we ask the world: What is it that you are up to?

Culturally I am also a person of variety. The culture of the island of Puerto Rico is made up of the following three peoples and their extensions: indigenous (Taino and through them the whole of the pre-Columbian American world), Spanish (which would include much that is from the Arabs, the Gypsies and, to some extent, the Jews) and the African (the greatest African influence in the Caribbean comes from the Yorubas). All these styles, rhythms and flavors—as I like to describe them—are in transit through each other, making interesting brews for poet and musician, for painter and dancer, for scholar and worshiper.

Because of our political situation as a territory of the United States, one of the last classic colonial holdings by an empire, we are also a people who live within a great cultural clash, a debate between values. This interlude between Anglo-North American and Hispano-Criollo Caribbean keeps all issues of identity intensive throughout the island and within all the Puerto Rican diaspora communities on the U.S. mainland. A great deal of my poetry has been written at the center of this intersection. Despite the fact that I am a bilingual poet writing in both Spanish and English, I do not advocate a bilingual atmosphere within this island of close to four million inhabitants, the majority of which cling to the Spanish tongue and live a cultural existence as a Hispano-Criollo Caribbean nation. The greater part of my work has been rendered in English, the English of my upbringing. I must point out here that bilingualism is closer to the norm than the exception as we run across the literatures of the world. Almost all the great writers throughout the ages have been involved in second languages, if not as users for sure as translators. Countries even have various levels of their languages: for instance, an urban Spanish, a countryside mountain Spanish. Jargon, slang. My poems are composed in both languages and not all the time do I use the language in which the thoughts were thought. Bilingualism is not a limitation when it is in the hands of the writers, but it will create confusion if a whole people is subjected to it at once. The two languages add to the expressive possibilities of my experiences, which are both lived and studied, or as Borges has put it in a poem: "for what the night and the books have given me."

I hope that these poems are useful. Useful even beyond a writer named Victor. Perhaps you will find revelations in its fleeting moments, ideas and feelings that might address your current position, the problems which you might be confronting, ideas about cultures and how they might coexist enjoying their best features. As I have mentioned, I am a body of migration, an entity of constant change. From a tropical village to the biggest urban center known to man, from the East Coast to the West, from Spanish to English, from spirit to flesh. Poetry lives between thought and music as a sonorous flickering bird. The poem is neither the words nor the letters, the poem is not the fibers of the pages of this book, nor the ink, a poem is an invisible sensation which surges from the depths of its occurrences into the light of understanding through language. If there were no languages, there would still be the poem. Exactly where does it come from? Don't ask me. I am merely a victim, perhaps from that other part of our minds which we borrow from the Gods.

The Guayabera
Is the Tuxedo
of the Caribbean

Snaps of Immigration

1

I remember the fragrance of
the Caribbean
A scent that anchors into the
ports of technology.

2

I dream with suitcases
full of illegal fruits
Interned between white
guayaberas that dissolved
Into snowflaked polyester.

3

When we saw the tenements
our eyes turned backwards
to the miracle of scenery
At the supermarket
My mother caressed the
Parsley.

4

We came in the middle of winter
from another time
We took a trip into the future
A fragment of another planet
To a place where time flew
As if clocks had coconut oil
put on them.

5

Rural mountain dirt walk
Had to be adjusted to cement
pavement
The new city finished the
concrete supply of the world
Even the sky was cement
The streets were made of shit.

6

The past was dissolving like
sugar at the bottom of a coffee cup
That small piece of earth that
we habitated
Was somewhere in a television
Waving in space.

7

From beneath the ice
From beneath the cement
From beneath the tar
From beneath the pipes and wires
Came the cucurucu of the roosters.

8

People wrote letters as if they
were writing the scriptures
Penmanship of woman who made
tapestry with their hands
Cooked criollo pots
Fashioned words of hope and longing
Men made ink out of love
And saw their sweethearts
Wearing yellow dresses
Reaching from the balcony
To the hands of the mailman.

9

At first English was nothing
but sound
Like trumpets doing yakity yak
As we found meanings for the words
We noticed that many times the
Letters deceived the sound
What could we do
It was the language of a
foreign land.

New/Aguas Buenas/Jersey

In the forties the populace was sucking on barb
wire
Cans found on the streets were squeeze to the
maximum
Hot air moving through wooden houses
They were Bohíos
We were Tainos
Its Areyto moving down from Sumidero
Pouring in from Caguitas
Inside the living rooms Aguasboneses walked
on compressed dirt
They made it shine
Cooked on kerosene stoves
Says the elders they woke up with stained noses
The chemical odor did them in
For that reason they lived in the streets
They lived in the mountains
Go home to eat and sleep
Roosters mounted chickens at random under
houses
For the children the toys were the insects
and sing songs from the time of Spain
Closer than Spain was the pain
People survived with the beauty of the song
The hidden gracious heart
That love that loved whoever it was
We carry our blood
Even towards destructions
And what else could it be
An army to fight destiny: for what in the matter
The families collapsed like red flowers
off of flamboyan trees.

The Spanish wanted gold first.
The priest wanted converts.
Sailors have always wanted pussy.

The Taino kingdoms melted in the mountains
The Areytos into the bone marrow to mix with
The juices of semen to that now generation
Our faces aboriginal designs

The island was purgatory
The retina saw in flora and fauna the spirit half
The same way a chest or a cross is visible
It was our materialism
The Spaniards came with so much embroidery
Our virgins were naked
This is a climate for flesh
Up in Mula thrown on a hammock receiving wind
upon my testicles
Aroma of azucena jumps only at night
The same as La Siciliana who only opens
within the darkness
In the eyes of the plaza I can still
see the nakedness pouring out
The heat invites us to take off our clothes
Imagine such polyester melted by the
primal sun

I am moving in the tensions with the tenses
History hanging within long skirts
The Black Virgin La Montserrate on a passage
Through the center of a town of wooden
Houses painted blue, green, yellow, pink,
orange
Black shawls and white hats
Join the rivers, the trees, the frogs,
and the rain which is about to fall
And the rain which is about to fall
Rain
In adoration of an image

The island was abandoned by history
Only the sun fell upon a coast of Sourtern

Spaniards who improvised a government
Accusing others of the crimes they committed
To settle Taino yucayeyes they went deeper
inland
With flashes of Moorish and Visigothic
harmonics
Made paths through the guayaba flavor

Avicenna and ibn 'Arabi in costume at the
festival Bomba y Plena
Pineapple in Baghdad Morococo

The silence of the past
Rules the manifestations of the future
The spirits are in charge here
Who comes through Guánica
Who comes through San Juan Bay
Who comes through airport
Doesn't know how ridiculous
the riddle can get

The space was exported
as industry was imported
The campesinos were taken into the future
There was only past and future
There was no now
The Marine Tiger left
Sumidero Mula Caguitas
La Pajilla El Guanabano
went to Newark Avenue
Bergen Montgomery
Grove
Sixth Street
There was nothing to do in Aguas Buenas
But to stare into the mountain Jagueyes
There was no government
No plans for agriculture
The plans were for tourist

and pharmaceutical companies
The people who dropped the bomb on
Hiroshima came from the North
The methods were different
but the clearing was the same
A beautiful house with no one in it

Jersey City take the path back
To the island of vegetation
Let us retrogress into the future.

Agriculture

It is raining up
Not water
But belly buttons in
The plaza.
I am telling you this—
2,000 I see near
The ceiba tree.
Consequently umbrellas
Should be horizontal mouths
Facing down and wide open
Abandon all function
Give in to the
Pleasures of reversed
Gravity to its dream,
A world between belt
And shirt
Where bellies were tied
Like balloons.
With a strong pull out of
The ground
Where earthworms
Are librarians
Giving it on loan
Guava with fishnet
Stockings—
This is all without
The slightest intention
Of music
Lyrics which will turn
Belly buttons into brushes
Painting circles—
As the insects cross
Into the vibration
Under the flight of
Invisible parrots

Which are parallel
To white dresses
Whose upper embroidery
Is a closed curtain
For dancing guanavanas.

Trio Los Eternos

I placed my hand upon your absence
and inquired as to your whereabouts
have you gone to Rome of Italy
for voluptuous decorations of verse
Have you gone to Miami to dance at
the Copacabana and later to dine
across the street at Versailles
its hungry world of mirrors
eating you up
Are you in the mouth of the
Persians composing an ode to
Black hair
Are you in the Spain of the
Arabs deciphering feminine eyes
Radiating through plazas of water
fountains with lines of orange
trees taking notes for a scholar
who will write two tomes on the
meaning of a single glance.

You tell me you have gone into
yesterday to approach the singers
who sang with their ears
Accompanied by guitars with legs
playing people sideways
You are within the memory and no
longer need the galloping paintings
that come upon horses of Paso Fino.

The lyrics of a song walk around
the entrance of the room where once
upon a time you dwelled
It was launched from another realm
to come get you
It was lost there

Dissolved
Like a tamarind ice cone
in the Sahara

You had gone to a world of dirt
and vegetable rhythms based on
the appearance of sunlight
To play with what appears out of
Appearance
Which is something from something
It just stood still for one
million years
Till storytellers arrived throwing
mountains here and there
Minerals started to run
like French whores

The moisture was such that it
leaned more towards liquid than air
And that's when the first fish announced
itself and insisted on coming to land
to buy a Panama hat from the
Handcrafters who moonlighted
chiseling symbols on clay and rock
Architects coming through wind
separating air.

The second time I saw you after
you disappeared you had a bottle
of rum and were rambling about
The earth being a place where you
pay fifteen minutes of pain for two
minutes of fun and this was
a ridiculous way to be
So you had another shot of rum
and brought down the celestial
Court

And not wanting to call dios
You substituted diez
And out there in Urugutun
Sons of whores multiplied
ten by shit.

Since you left to yesterday
The birds still make their landings
customary upon the sugar language
of once songs
Everything that was: is
Insects and birds tell that the
dead still get their coffee at
three o'clock
Humanity thinks it is a simple
ritual of the birds to land
on your balcony every day
Till that beautiful day of summer
when you came back
You appeared dressed in black
Declaiming poetry in a little town
of the Americas—the sweet bread
The plaza
Events and things circulating
Coming out in different shapes
In many everywheres
The air evaporates
As motion goes backwards
San Juan Bautista runs out of
the water thousands baptized
Never looking back
For a yesterday that is today.

Al-Haram

(The red one)

The red one will come through letter and number
As I flip the Spanish cards linked to the
Egyptian Tarot
She will be an equestrian
Galloping upon a flying horse

The hidden
Red pepper
In a stew
Not the thing itself
But the shadow

She sometimes appears in green
but I know it is a disguise
For I come from the land of
Interior decorators
I have spotted her pushing
Her way out of purple and pink
A clear sign that she is going home
She is nowhere if she is not there
There is only one place

That place is protected by the
Sound the color makes
A red drum from Loíza Aldea
Directs traffic at the corner

It's in fowl play too:
What came first the chicken or
The egg
Answer: The rooster
Who entered quietly into the
Chicken coop
To deplume red feathers

It is night tight
The best time
Half in dream
She goes under
The Red Sea

She is coming through the
Undercurrent
Its pull irresistible
An echo becomes form in space
There is no water for the thirst
For the satisfaction is fire

She is walking 8,000 miles away
from where I am airing
Out of a window
She is in Cidra walking down
one of its small streets
Each step she takes
Drops a piece of her body
Till finally she is only
The virtues of the hue
Crimson on the great horizon

Glances and walks
Of the pensamiento
Come to the cherry entrance
Where they bow
with the rest of the aspirants

The red face is turning
Like dice turning onto four
Multiplication brings it to
Me more
It is raining blood
In the town between two
Mountains

Al-Haram lives there—
Find her door and bring
Midnight serenade
Lyrics and guitars below
Balcony
Minds disappear from the present
Go for walks under orange trees
Passage through sea coast
Red sails to Red

Al-Haram
Travels like pollen
Grows in invisibility
Notice at night
Starring into the darkness

That she comes
As a shrimp taken by the river
Is history
As prescribed by the doctors

Succumb to my painting
For there are no exits
The red fog is coming down from
The hills to suffocate us—

As the hands of a thief of calling
Seizes the gold
So will my hands
Open the porton of the red one's
Balcony

Its combination
The number
The code
Broken

A brown hand leans upon a white
Wall

As if pushing it away—
The body making a house
Where the guest enters
To find ferocious animals
Tamed and loose in the backyard.

Scarlet Skirt

I terminated with the color red
when this vibrant hue pressed against
me up on a mountaintop
Upon which I didn't know how I got
Drunk and in pursuit of a scarlet
skirt that had made a passage through
a festive plaza
It started the way it started
but don't ask me how that was
Rum and 98 degrees is a devastation
of the senses
Through her lips she gleamed a yes
And with that yes we went off on
a journey onto a street to the point
where cement ran out
And the red dirt began
The night was choking the daylight
out of the atmosphere
You could still count the coquís
which had started their nightly
Glee club
We didn't hold hands
But in the sway of the walk our pinkies
would brush against each other
In midair
She told me her name but it was
already the point when the bottle
Of rum was beyond the halfway mark
So all I could do now is speculate
Was it Nilsa, or Elena or Julia
Just plain and thrown
Or was it Anna-María, Sonia Carmin
Something with more combustive
Syllables
Or was it a much more rural name

Like Blasina or Amparo
It is all now in the flow of the
river that we might have passed
En route towards a singular light
At the very top of the earth
Which was her house
This part of the path was full
Of rocks which turned out to be
frogs
For they would take leaps
In front of my foolish head
Which by now had more rum
Than the bottle
The sounds of animals
The soft breeze
The crescent moon
Convinced us to sit on a
fallen tree
Her legs dispersed out of
her scarlet skirt in various
Curves
As we spoke little episodes
of our histories
I shot flurries of warm moisture
into her ears
And then as quick as a lizard's
head she stood up
Saying I must go
disappeared into the darkness
The tail of a cow which had
been watching us from a distance
Did more than us
There I was in the sullen shade
of night holding an empty
Bottle of rum far from the
center of town in an elevation
Which I knew not

Composing myself I threw the bottle
away and took direction
My head in the misty heaven of
sugar cane
Singing the opening lines of one
bolero after another
Lo I came upon a fork in the road
Going is never like coming
A pause of indecision
The whole Caribbean stood still
I just went in the direction I heard
less frogs and coquís
Thinking myself en route towards
civilization
After some paces I found the hole
of my life
I fell down a precipice like
a clown in a movie
With my white apparel I cleaned
the side of the mountain
And fell into a gathering of
guava bushels
There I was drunk and dizzy
crimson from the mud I had
Rolled on
I shitted twice on the cipher 10
and continued my journey into
Town
At long last I found the lights
of the beginning
Soon I was crossing the plaza
It must've been one in the morning
I looked like a potato that had
been internalized in a pot of
Red beans
I made a turn on the street
leading to my home

Suddenly I saw a figure of
good dimensions standing next
To the gate
It was not human but a beast
I came a little closer and
registered that it was in fact
A bull
Tremendous bullshit
I found a rock and threw it in its
direction to see if it would scatter
Away
But it was immobile
It just stood there waiting as
if I owed it some money
I had to find an alternate way
of getting to my bed
I went through a side street
and climbed the stairs of
Don Berencho's house which gave me access
to the roof of the house next to
mine
This put me in jumping distance
onto the back balcony of my house
I swore that I had left the door
open
Once I jumped and turned the knob
it told me something else
It had been closed
I thought of yelling to my sister
But I reviewed my condition
Drunk
Bumps and scratches all over
And my clothes looked as if I'd
just climbed out of a pot of
Red beans
What words could be occupied as
an explanation?

I laid myself out on an old
rattan sofa that we had there
The thought of the scarlet skirt
beat me to sleep
It is such an expensive color
its the heat of our passions
I terminated with the color red
After descending from the
mountaintop.

Mithra

Persia is sprinkling through
the sun upon the beaches
Of Cabo Rojo
Ten thousand people dressed
in white disappear
Into the solar arms
Rising they turn into
the pages of
Chilam Balam
Words printed on sheets
of gold
Hung upon mountains of rock
Out of which they made
Mayagüez
The plaza crumbling beneath the
weight of benches
Where giant birds were landing
To rest
As they were en route to
la India
Sitaring the chords of light
for Vilmiki to see
Straw hats walking an Ox
Across the River Guaranile
Out of the sand Mithra singers
rise and their heads grow horns
The heat in chorus changes
the tongue:

Mitra
Ven y Ven y Ven
Tu lámpara pa luz
Está aquí
Tu sueno de fuego
con cama al lado del mar

Te recibiré en seda azul
Mitra
Ven y Ven y Ven
Pal suelo a bailar
Luego te mandamos para
Atrás en alas de golondrinas

Lindas gracias
Por tu medalla que brilla
Mitra
Ven y Ven y Ven
Derrite estos zapatos
Y luego los pies
Escribe en la arena
Este acto de fe
Cuerpos en la playa
Achiote cubierto en blanco
Papel
Mitra Ven y Ven y Ven
Anterior a Roma
Antes de Jerusalem
De los señores el señor
Máquina que al suspirar
Prendio el aire con fuego
En la noche tranquila
La que viene
La que fue
La que es
Mitra Ven y Ven y Ven

The sand turns red hot
Sparkling
The ocean is gasoline
The dancers catch fire
As it starts to rain
Machetes.

Christianity

Christianity
sparkling from pentecostal
Rhythm
Coming as if a mouth
Up from
Calle San Lazaro del Medio
Timbal and maraca with
tambourine inviting San Pedro
Horse to gallop
Through hair and flesh
Like needles of chill
Pulling down Jehovah
with a singsong
Those beautiful faces that
I saw bopping a wooden church
Gone was the whole place
With white dresses—guayaberas
of grace
Out towards doubtless space
I threw myself in with that
and kneeled next to a picture
Of María with a child
In her arms
A maternal embrace
Taking care of you.

Islam

The revelation of the revelation
The secrets offered in rhythms
The truth of heaven entering through
chorus
Yourself runs into yourself
Through a crack of understanding
As if Falcons landed on a
shoulder of your thoughts
With a letter from your guardian
angel—
Like Caribbean mambo dancers
The whirling dervishes go off
spinning into the arms of light
Across a floor of endless squares
and circles
Calligraphy brushed into tiles
Painted inside the names of God
Love
Compassion.

Chronic Chronicles

The buccaneers used to rub her belly
In search of the brilliant gold emanation
A life in search of thrill and
loose merchandise
Sailing the wind of destiny
Sabers of pure white soul giving
off flame in the night
East Trade Wind surfers
For whom the stars have telephones
Dutch and munching 16-letter words
In guava land
Shapes light that Rembrandt can
take back
And throw between the opening of a
tree
A slight maneuver to stare at
the lasting of time
They starred as if they arrived in
heaven
The splendor of the mountains
Pregnant with flora the daughter of
Hurakán the wind and the waters of
The blessing
Tribe by tribe told their stories
to the strangers
After they got through the sound of their
tongues
Pointing and waving hands at each other
On the beach making designs on the sand
It was summer for ever
Carib-Siboney-Taino nudity camps
Out of between mountain villages
Where from palm roofs the smell of
Fish and pineapple
That's why standing in this town

of Spanish plaza watching the habitants
Sweat the heat I want to yell at top
voice The Tainos were correct Señores
Y Señoras feel this heat let us everyone
and each take off our clothes
The nun and the priest
The barber and the hatmaker
The tobacconist and the charlatan
All simultaneously skin naked appear
Erase this Christian fear
From island where the rocks talk to
you
And the leafs have fingers
A town built on native huts
Bone of the ancient memory glitters
in our eyes
Was it my neighbor that met the Spanish
guitar
Hurried to the coast to dance flamenco
Doña Aljedrez
The one of black embroidered shawl
Don Gallego who keeps fighting roosters
and duels in the town with anyone
The ones of brave silence
Who still sleep the cock's song
The tobacco rollers who weave in
stories lies and in poetry of
Memory and rhyme declare themselves
The owners of truth
One of them ran into Ponce de León
who was contemplating his wrinkled
Hands and as a way to get him out of
Town pointed north towards a Fountain
of Youth
His tale went into his tail
The sails become another dot on the blue page
of Caribbean sky

Everyone has come and gone
Through these islands of the transients
following rumors and pictures of progress
Like gusts of wind beings have taken flight
British and Dutch hungry on the coast
The shine of golden bells atop
church steeples guides them in
1621 year the Dutch attacked San Juan
and made a mess of the cobblestone streets
The white Andalusian homes splattered
with blood
Screams through the fans
The criollos defend their homes
Held their own
The Dutch into the sea jump
Taking the Golden Bell of the Cathedral
to Amsterdam
Months later while residents cleaned
up
As if a double-Dutch treat a Hurricane
is spotted forming with an anger known to
the wind
Into the new city it came and combed
all hair atop all head
A hiss from God's throat
The city is busy with action
Everything arrives with force

The purity of air was such
That months before the Spanish
Saw land their odor permeated the
East Trade Winds
In the dreams of the wise priest
they made images
In consul they were discussed
Cacique and priest exchanged notes
Their voices keeping children awake

behind the palm walls
The fascination of the strange
A human affair
Through the ages making history
unite
Seashells were blown when the sails
were spotted
The note made an echo through
the mountainous verdal
Out to greet the bearded
Came the well versed.

Tradición

Let the water rain into the forest
So that the vines holding up the güiros
Can flourish
Craft attack the vegetable kingdom
And make the lines that will sound
In Baltasar's ears
On the day of the astrologers
Along with the guitar of the
fourth dimension
Those that know themselves within: dance
Those that know themselves within: song
Those that know themselves within: relations
Those that know themselves within: food
Those that know themselves within: Religion
Those that know themselves within: Prayer
Those that know well the place of their tongue
The shape of their sound
Can go then and make everything disappear.

Corsica

Underneath with the geologic plates
Puerto Rico and Corsica
Are holding hands
Both hands with gold rings
Sweating each other's palms
The same moon is seen
From both islands
The light of the sun
Upon the mother
The seaman's stories of migration
Like whispering olives within
Red beans
Inhabit the seasonings
Echoing through the island
Cave's fifth aboriginal dimension
Of Camuy
Where not far from the salt
Of the sea
The compass of the fishing
Boats zero in on Minerva's
Lips of crimson shine
Who are flowing in the currents
Of the river within the ocean
Inviting the estrangement of
The planet to come and sit
In the plazas—the delights of
Sweet breads and virginal circular
Night walks of white dresses
Ah, Minerva blessed was your
Father at the thought of Migration
It was the limestones of the
Caverns speaking underground
You are now as a
Mediterranean sway en route
Equatorial

With Manatí pineapples lit
Electrical down Antillean
Street aflame
Palés Matos following you
With his eyes of drumming sounds
Crazy
This is Corsica
Puerto Rico is in the Mediterranean
All the eyes are the same.

Problems with Hurricanes

A campesino looked at the air
And told me:
With hurricanes it's not the wind
or the noise or the water.
I'll tell you he said:
it's the mangoes, avocados
Green plantains and bananas
flying into town like projectiles.

How would your family
feel if they had to tell
The generations that you
got killed by a flying
Banana.

Death by drowning has honor
If the wind picked you up
and slammed you
Against a mountain boulder
This would not carry shame
But
to suffer a mango smashing
Your skull
or a plantain hitting your
Temple at 70 miles per hour
is the ultimate disgrace.

The campesino takes off his hat—
As a sign of respect
towards the fury of the wind
And says:
Don't worry about the noise
Don't worry about the water
Don't worry about the wind—

If you are going out
beware of mangoes
And all such beautiful
sweet things.

To El Grupo Folklórico y Experimental Nuevayorquino

for Andy and Jerry Gonzalez

Translation: Vision-Version:

This is a poem that combines
the memories of several cultures into one unique juice.

Its language is that of songs
because the poem tries to approximate the lyrical
presentations of this musical group.

Their name is of the utmost interest and central
to this poem—though it is only used directly
in the title.

Folklore and Experiment: They are well rooted in
their house which is an evolutionary spiraling
movement reaching out and incorporating all sounds
with a brilliance that can flicker in all the
streets of human cities.

Their music is compared to color
though no specific color is mentioned for in their
case that would be a limitation of locale. All
true scholars know that parts of humanity have
only recently awakened those areas of their brains
which inform them of wonderful tinges. Pupils see
and learn: their music brings us in front of hidden
air of the rainbow.

There is a sense of history in this tribute when
it mentions ships, islands, tropical vistas (country-
sides), jets, transportation of human aspirations
from one geographical area to another and instead

of this process being detrimental is used—turned
around in a sense—giving a crystal knowledge to
all creatures, now that it is all here what do we
do. Go with it, back and forth, present it side-
ways, start in the middle, walk with your back for-
ward to where the original telephones were still
plugged to roots (routes) Heartbeat-Footsteps-Breath
through thyroid (the Will) larynx (vocal chords)
A mention is made of them having their ears (DOORS)
on the lookout for the hissings and rumblings of
Gods (Creative Energy).

The Mayas knew and accepted that all human beings
are antennas—thus roots of the universe—through
their insight into sound and adherence of the law
of the clave, the three-two beat

ʼ ʼ ʼ ʼ ʼ
ʼ ʼ ʼ ʼ ʼ

the men and women who form this group are true
honorables of that system of being.
The final correspondence between musicians and
poet(s) gives a sense that what was being written
came from an alphabet that was being taken out
from the center of a sky within the sea.

Note: El Grupo Folklórico y Experimental Nuevayorquino
has two albums out to date:
Concepts in Unity (Salsoul Records: Sal-2-400)
Lo Dice Todo (Salsoul Records: Sal-4110)

Messages from Across the Street
on Tobacco and Water Wires

The ocean turned red
And the land turned blue
Your face became a sensation
Your features were eaten by the
ground
Your tears reentered the breasts
of the mothers of singers
The fado
The bolero
El canto hondo
The sadness
the lament
The nostalgia
The separation

The rumbling of your heart
The dancing of your feet
Will circulate within the pockets
of the wind
Your hate will make a shadow
That covers the flowers in chill

You will not be forgotten
Plant your seed well
It is the harvest you will pick

It will be beautiful
You will have no mouth to keep shut
Starring will turn into cha-cha-chá
The craters of the moon will be
full of guayaba juice

We speak here the word which is spirit
Those on the other side tell me they speak
in matter

Out of pure air comes objects
Vegetable gases minerals can flow
In combination
And you can make a hammock
Between Uranus and Mars
Where a puff of love can swing

The watches and clocks go backwards
It is 13 o'clock out there
Your pain becomes currency
To buy the harmony of Celina

The ocean turns red
The boats are made of fire
Allan Kardec is the
Captain
Of one of them

His passengers come for water
on the shore
They marvel at the blue sand they
Will never step on
From your prayers they make
a picture of your face
So with confidence give it to
the worms
Leave your smile on endless loan
In the sensational land you are
going to you can kiss without lips
The history of your life
will be in the fingertips of the drummers
Nothing was wasted
Even the blank moments when we are

Morons
Drunks help us get home
The tears are the milk of the drummers
also
They sing and play
Your laughter
Your joy
Your dancing
The nostalgia
The separation

Libros

This is a leaf
It is from the palms
That the river of words
is entering the valley
Into the caves
the winds of hurricanes
Chasing the crabs
of the oceans
Leafs hanging in the
wind are the archives
Of the gone
Exchanges between thought
and fingers
In the landscape
alphabet of rocks
The library of Alexandria
emptied into a Bedouin
guitar
Sprayed from the desert
Into flamenca's eyes
Who sailed the Atlantic
To make the pineapples
compose coplas
Upon sheets of golden
sun rays
So hot that insects want
to take off their clothes
And just be whispers
writing out of palms.

An Essay on William Carlos Williams

I love the quality of the
spoken thought
As it happens immediately
uttered into the air
Not held inside and rolled
around for some properly
schemed moment
Not sent to circulate a cane
field
Or on a stroll that would include
the desert and Mecca
Spoken while it happens
Direct and pure
As the art of salutation
of mountain campesinos come to
the plaza
The grasp of the handshake upon
encounter and departure
A gesture unveiling the occult
behind the wooden boards of
your old house
Remarks show no hesitation
to be expressed
The tongue itself carries
the mind
Pure and sure
Sudden and direct
like the appearance
of a green mountain
Overlooking a town.

Theory of Why the Night Comes

The blue sky gets tired
The silver light of the moon
turns into a broom
And starts sweeping blue
sheets
Slowly the horizon changes
into a nightgown
And jumps over the moon
Into the mouth of the sun
Which takes it with it
To fry bamboo shoots
in China.

Versions of Basho in Spanish

El lago de siempre.
Mira a un sapo—
Agua por doquiera.

El viejo lago—
Sapo de momento
Se mojo la cosa.

Lago
Sapo
Fua
Agua.

An Evening on the River Ganges

Sugar is also a color
The tongue can see its appearance
Between meditation and dance
A serious blast to the tongue
The Milky-Way musical bar
A sensational space it left
To arrive in the earth of grasshoppers
Nothing can tie sweetness down
A taste from beyond
In the Ganges the sweet and sour
Bones baptize their journey
Thought goes to the feet along
Its banks of cool wet
The sun through silk
Like water through coffee beans
Like cold coconut milk
Down inferno throat
Satan runs on fire
Chased by peeled mangoes
Into the forest
All the trees start talking
The Devil stores the stories
Ganges flowing from the feet
Till it breaks into ocean mind
It takes it light now
Thrown on sofas
Embracing the queen of curves
The hug with all six arms
She whispers:
Some are jumping from event to event
All this history is coming
But with our desire
Let us first make the sky
Forces sitting down like pupils
River water coming to the sea

This is the inception
The words without poets
Later you'll run into the tigers
Dancing out of their flesh
Diving and vaulting into the Ganges
Coming out electric wet
Shipping each bone of your spine
towards the lyrics
There a balcony and a palace
Buddha's ex-wife bracelets anklets
Cymbals pirates mothers gypsies
Wondering nations of columns
Visitations of milk queens
With moisturizing looks that
Kings send for
Their feet bottoms of red achiote
Dancing Rama-cha-cha
Collapsing
Fainting in front of the fresh water
I call her name as the fragrance
Of café awakens me into the
Puerto Rican Aguas Buenas morning
Where across the street
My grandfather Julio El Bohemio
Made cigars once
Eternally.

Heart Surgery

Shiiist—like a bullet
I turn the light off
You say it was the sun—
But I know it was your face
Your stare is like an
encyclopedia
I can look up anything
I want.
If you were a rose
Like old boleros declare
have you not heard:
Rose of my garden
I will guard you till
you have grown and make
For you in heaven a throne—
Your lips made of rose petals
whispering into my soul—
I would walk into paradise
and pick you thorns and all—
And throw you into the wind
then with a telescope in my hands
Go after you like the Arecibo
Observatory pulling down the
firmament
Spot your spot
And dive a million miles
Towards the center
In six seconds—
Otherwise I might fall in love—
And will be taken out of
reality as in an ambulance
Towards the hospital
of hard sad truth
Vomiting the desperate
loneliness of separation

And betrayal—
For what good are we then
An empire ceases to exist
Might as well string out
like clothes in tenements
of melancholy lines
Crumbled and broken into pieces—
ready for the broom and the
final disposal—
How could love fall into
itself
Stay where you are sunrise
Drinking memories
Just once the sweet illusion
comes
Just once do you fall so hard
That some of the pieces
disappear—
Just once do you love in
life—
Remember the song
which comes from eternity
To wake you up—
Like a bullet I turn the
light off
You say it was the sun
But I know that the tears
that are falling from my eyes
Are drying upon the laughter
of my lips.

Contradictions

If you are chilly
You are hot.

Poesia Tropical for You

Lavender the color and
the fragrance emitting
out of flora radio
With a mountain that
is walking towards the
Atlantic
Spiders who scatter
like a charge of electricity
Over a white wall in a
White house that dances
towards green bananas and
Papayas as avocados throw
Their hands in an attempt
to walk the house around
a river
Unto the other side
Where oranges have within
them the memory of silk
And sandals walking
under pagodas reading
The scrolls of Mencius
Holding Carolina's hair
of black Mandarin
Everywhere the air hot
and opened
As the slant of the eyes
produce
Verses which are being
carried
Like dust sprinkled upon
the backs of lizards
Towards the seashells
The memories of vistas
of land
In motion out of blue water.

The Coconut Clock

By spacing the counted moments of
appearance as it presents itself in
Places
By celestial plan-ification
We happened both at the post office
line.
Sending mail and boxes off to different
infinities
Specific Caribees—
Her wonder made her play with her
hair
The vein of love riding through
the juices of the nerves
Despite herself she flies
For that very reason I have become
Space

The air is a radio transmitting
as if surprised at surprise
Somewhere inside that vision is
a group of numbers adding up,
Shy to rise her eyes directly
As her fingers no longer hers
Whirlpool endless black curls.

Her features
Migration Catalan infused with
Caribbean tribes
Her nose the superior of the blend
Nostalgia native
Pride installed in flesh
A yellow with a spray of red

A painting of a first orgasm
Appears in memorial fountain

Her face blushes rushes rosy
A journey from the tinge of papaya
That has shifted into hazelnut

As the rooster and chicken leave
the small tile of encounter,
At the post office
The correspondence goes off.

Jíbaro Scientific Axiom

A quarter-pound of shit

Weighs more than 100 pounds of coffee

Weather Report

Pushing light out of town
That from morning has been leaning
Upon roofs and balconies
Sun for which we are frying pan
For which we love despite the burn

Even after it has gone down it is still
Yelling and jumping onto our hair
Our necks, shoulders
Finally the invading army of night
Coolness conquers our territory
We rest hammock-ally to contemplate
That tomorrow
The town will be set on fire again.

Igneris

Air is raining upon the organs
of reproduction
From heaven the color spectrum
into your pelvis
Raining a ceremony of structures
Upon the joys of the winds.

This is the drum of my island
The coast of an eternal circle
I sea it in the wheres I follow
Hear it in the hands that designate
Upon the skin of a goat stretched
In the sun maps for the knee and ankles
To join the trunk of the trees
That the barrel was made from.

El Yunque is falling into necks
and waists appearing in dreams.
With nature you dance
Get in rhythm Catalan, Galician,
Asturians bow to the vegetable
Instruments that rattle indigenous
Joints to sour and disappear
Through doors found in echoes.

That's the juice
Before Spain the snake dance
The waist in the river woman
Bells and flute caracoles
Caracoles sipping the dawn
Guayaba painting the insect wings
Flavor colors
Earth Igneri
AguasBuenas
Guesbuenas
Agueybanás

Deep in the caves I grow
In light light
Where rodents fly
Oxygen to fish that shell
Their coats and hats
Radios in their bellies
Where lightning falls

Phosphorous La Parquera is
a light bulb in the mar
When she was a virgin
It was seen from the moon

She knew how to melt rocks for
Perfume
Importing it beyond registered
frequencies—
To make a brown so round
That before it was seen
Shape was heard

Sonadora was not cement and cal
boxes
It was just an opening
A musical
A song is heard out of the flora
The hum of love
The moan of two
Tree comes in fauna

Now Igneris flames upon cement
the trail of a soul
Religion is a God that moves the
Feet
Scratches backs and tabs shoulders
Up on the stage presents
Itself in costumes

Which shows how to progress
Walking inside.

I got source and can shake it off
To sprinkle the designs
That hide the patterns
Of the lord of movement
I am the explosion of the fiesta
The timing of feet and elbows
The moisture of lips sacrosanct
Manifesting the evidence of presence
The heart speaking in the hands
Before it grows wings to land again
Upon the supply.

Creole Eyes

It was about to rain
The day became dark clouds
Wind escaping from pockets
Above the mountains
It was grey and cloudy
And then I saw the sun—
That is the one of prominent eyes
Of native features
Of full body
Soft and with a melody
Of walk composed of guitar
And fruit and nights of sleeping
By a river's flow
Grace and walk

Has she broken from her grandmother who
Accompanies her to church on Sundays
To light candles to the saints
Has she found her own world
Beyond the mountains is she she?

Or is she of the human frozen
Habitual gestures
Riding along with time without
Stopping
Nodding in the plaza

But no
Let us call her fire
Because she stopped the rain
The motion of respiration
Why pay taxes to pave the
Streets
Which she breaks every day
She walks by.

Encomiendas

When they distributed my blood
To the conquering material
Divided as if we didn't have
A plan divine
An invisible organization
I stayed out of the imposition
By making an ultraviolet
Bohío next to a river
Where I heard the flow of stories
And saw light the way you
Feel the sun at night
For my dwelling is the senses
Of creation
My circle poetic Areyto
My helpers live under rocks
Inside caves
Atop mountains
I am doing now
What I did then—
Creating the story of my journey
In words
Watching from a distance
The continuation of nothing
As the plumes fan out
To celebrate the fluid contents
Emanating from the heritage.

Conduits of Sound

A bridge made of perfume
Was what I took to step out
Where I blossomed as sculpture
In the form of words
Uttered by a lover—
At the fulfillment of the dream,
Kissing an ear with a hanging caracol
Vocals now lost for duration
Knowing that I left friends
On the bridge—
Who are walking
The patchouli towards
Your shoulder.

Three Movements

1 El Indio – Movimientos

Estoy persiguiendo tus huellas
tus ojos

The stars guide red bones out of
caves
Appearing before the moon
They immediately recognized their
home
And gave it a system of sounds

Going around like curves were
flashes of thought
The homes became round
And dance took its shape
From the highest to the
bottom
Like orbits of the blood-
stream
Circles of the dance
Disc of the sun
Opening of the mouth

THE SONG THAT DANCES ARE MY BOOKS
Covering corners of memories
Like bricks laid within
Painted cubbyholes marks
A fine map out of space
For those who know
That life is waking dream
In the airways between the stars
The procession of spirits
Animation straight up
The eye still swimming in moisture

SIGHT WAS PRAYER

2 España Spain

Conquer-conquerre conquista
Inquisition
Conquering conquista
Allah chased the Visigoths
to the Pyrenees
Where for 800 years they
stared at rocks
Fans of knowledge opened
in Cordova Granada
There was peace and discourse
Some Visigoths came back
and learned
Medicine and how to play guitar

HISPANIA
Falling into Africa
of the North
Now your eyes are
dark
And your hands walk upon
strings
I say that you are also a door
Cultural spirits go in and out
Flavors reach their destination
Whole bodies were stolen by
Gypsies and made to dance

Andalusia
The earth of which
Harvests poets
Who are given words by
fervent souls
Describing settings not here yet
"The eye cannot see the essential things"

Out of the blue they came

To where the seashells made echoes
Things have never been the same

ESPAÑA CONQUEST CONQUER
Conquering
Hispania the hidden will now
arise
With red clay on its face.

3 Africa—Choreo Thoughts

The mother of metaphor
For sound is deciphered to
Specific meaning
Nature is made to obey
The rhythm of a voice
Or the hands upon a drum
Within a prior consent
of the cosmos
The man and woman that knows
the alphabet
Can speak the letters
It is a way of being
That stayed strongly itself
within the Catholic Hispanas
It can change shapes and names
while the inside stays the same

AFRICA IS CALLING ME LIFTING UP MY FEET

The holy rhythm
The rhythmic soul of the Caribbean

THE CONGA IS A TELEPHONE
R I N G
BOMBA PU TA KA TA BUUM
BOMBA PU TA KA TA BUUM

From New Orleans
To Tango land
In Vera Cruz and Ecuador
In Cartagena and Lima Peru
Africa has in each place a home

INDIO AFRO HISPANO
Along Andalusian Spanish
In Chicago San Francisco and

New York
We carry a treasure within
to cherish and preserve
But most important to EXPRESS.

Was Is

Greetings this is the echo of the disappeared
Intersection blood
Out of space transmitting
The glitter of red gold
The meaning of hieroglyphs
The drumming of the heart
The dance feat of poetry song
The messages from the skies
Deposited into your eyes
Greetings from my bush of voices
From the flora of sounds
From the maleza of images
I am the spirit
Which is now touch
I am the substratum
Invisible in the textbooks
I am what's walking yet not seen
Bursting is the sweetness
behind the salt
This is the witnesses of
clay and shellfish
Of azul waters rising
As my canoe feasting upon motion
Leaving behind alligators
Octopuses in pursuit
Before a rock I roll
As time blows into shape
The limestones of the caves
The language of commanded chance
Where the turtles gesture towards
The rosy sensations of my thoughts
Mandala bellies strolling museum
beaches
Laughter out of nowhere is the
presence of the station of the

Chiefs of tobacco pipes in jaws
That decipher ultimatums of comets
Rattling upon the necklaces of
virgins dancing in the stream
Between the eyes secret fountain
Greeting this is star feathers
Raining upon Areyto plazas
Calling you now
From your window of street today
Calling you now
Out of your Foreign berserk
Calling you now in Castilian or King's
English
Calling you now to abandon
Empty utterances
For the royal crown behind
Motion
Of the real oasis
The water falling from the gourds
Baptizing you

Calling
In a forever speech of colors
Calling you
Over the horizon
YUCA
YUCA
The gates of Yukiyu
A brilliant fire
Greetings.

Areyto

My empire of flamboyans
Through boulevards made of mountains
Dressed green to the heavens
As voices circulate the hymns
of our history
From the dancers of the round
serpent formed at the center of
Life
This is Americas Areyto
This is Americas Areyto

In cities mountains of flying metallic
cars and consumer junk/
Nerves piled up upon horizons
of progress
That whisper inside/
Mira look
Look mira that whisper inside
Is the old calendar ticking
The Areyto is still swinging:
The Gods said they would take
us back and deliver us from
Plush media inventions
From racket and industrial tension
From textbooks that are lying
tongues of pretensions
The river on the other side
of English is carrying the message
Yukiyu has not abandoned you
The quetzals are still flying
Quetzalcóatl is on the phone
Be cool Roberto and José
Carmen and María
Just go horizontal into the circle
Areyto

The current will take you

America that Betances, José Martí
That Hostos wanted all together as
ONE
Vasconcelos said RAZA CÓSMICA
Seeing red mixed with black
And black with white
Rhythms united married in history
This is the greatest flavor
The earth has to offer

Marimba tango samba
Danza Mambo bolero

Linda America just rise and take
off your clothes
Your age is so old that
Giants appear out of trees as tobacco
smoke takes photographs of the wind
Directing itself into a voice
Where salt pebbles dance guaguancó
Something so good that it became
blueprint for legs
That moved with such precision
That ten thousand appear to be one
In the Areyto where you hear the drum
As the knees and the legs
describe an area between two stars

Old fire of agricultural guitar
spreading North
Trio Los Diamantes sunrise moving
through silk on slow tropical wind
Johny Albino Trio San Juan
Making an escalator of sound
Into your hearts that grow feathers

79

To fly towards the desert to enter
The la'uds invasion of Iberian perfume
To land upon the shoulders of Gypsies
and Mayas as a fan from Granada cools
our Amerindian features of the love
That comes of the love that goes

America is our belly
Our abdomen of spirit
We grew out of the plants
It knows who we are
Linda America that Betances
José Martí to Hostos us up UNIDOS
As único one (JUAN)

America sur south
America norte
Juan America
Two America Juan
Juan America one
Then America blend
Give the idea roots of
harmonious peace serene/
Sí and yes it is possible for the
Snake of heart and mind to
grow quetzal feathers and fly
Out of the Areyto circle
Areyto circle
Areyto dance

Possible to be possible
Possible to be
A whole unto one
A nation with lots of fish to
eat
And fruit that offers itself
it is possible to be

it is possible to
Struggle against blocks
of inertia
Against conquistadors' wishes
lurking in blood nervous system
Nightmaring dreams/
Dogs that come bark at the
beautiful dance
It is possible to be
pure fresh river water
We are bird that sings
Free

Areyto
Maraca güiro and drum
Quicharo maraca y tambor
Who we are
Printed in rhythm and song

Areyto south
Areyto North
Two America Juan
One America One
America that Bolívar Betances
to José Martí Us to Hostos who wanted
us to be one único Unidos

Areyto güiro and drum
Quicharo maraca y tambor

Areyto song
Areyto song
AREYTO.

Good Waters

We do not claim to be of the fallen
The tradition of Agueybaná was not
Just within the material
It was not just in the people physical
In rhythm it is what still dances
In gene Plazas
Orbiters of extraction
Luminers of the messages in songs
The laws of travel
The events of the trajectory
How we formed in the interior
The round Bohiós
Which became the shape of our
Transmitting dance
Back home—shakers of maracas

Do not talk of things that do not
exist
The presence is the presence
Claim for good the good of the good
What have we gained?
From the lost of the good to the
Out of step
And what out of goodness it was
That now the horizon vegetation
Chokes and the coming progression
Has no water or air
The tradition wanted more good for
The good to distribute throughout
Without finishing the spot—
It knew that beyond the needs there
Was no need to progress into that
Up-tempo pace impossible to dance
That's the "one voice to call back
the good of the good we have lost"

Even such that comes to your tongue
That too is there
No matter what or where
Acá or Allá
For conflict nuts
Say: Adjuntas and Chicago

We do not claim to be of the fallen
We are still delivering sound in red packages
Upon this there was only an attempt
At something happening
At the edge of realization

We are still waiting
We have not fallen.

The Troubadour's Heritage

An older man beat me to the lyric—
When across the plaza
Swayed the loveliest damsel
That reality could produce
I started to combine phrases
In my mind
When Don Paco the Owl
Who rhymes at 85
Uttered in her listening distance
A single word:
Descansa—Rest he said
And I much younger and in my
Epoch of gold
Took back my poetry
And put it away.

Never a word so precious
and precise has been uttered
Exactly above a whisper
Three portions of air
The *Des* becomes a hiss at its
Finality
Where the center enters
The *can* which seems
To draw back in particles
Of the desired object
As it roles back out before
Falling into darkness
Helping to form the *sa* that
Banks at the roof of the mouth
And sprays out
It is that which now resounds
Within her memory.

Morning Rooster

Mountains in the North:
Hispanic Writing in the U.S.A.

The earth is migration, everything is moving, changing interchanging, appearing, disappearing. National languages melt, sail into each other; languages are made of fragments, like bodies are made of fragments of something in the something. Who'd want to stand still, go to the edges where you see clear the horizon, explore the shape of the coast? Are poets not the antennas of the race? Then tune into the chatter, the murmur that arises from the collection. Add and subtract, submit it to your mathematics. Take and give. Enlarge, diminish. The Romans ate everything up and now we dance Latin to African music, so we don't exactly fall into the things through the words. Columbus thought he came to the land of India and he even mistook Cuba for Japan. Language is clarification of the inner, of the part that does not rot. Moving through a terrain, languages would sound out gradation scale – Italian, Spanish, Portuguese – and so move through the whole planet making a tapestry. Old geography lingers in the language of the conquistadores: names of rivers and fruits. Our Spanish – which has Latin and Italian – has Taino, Siboney, Chichimeca. It has sounds coming out of it that amaze it and over the years it has been spiced, making it a rich instrument full of our history, our adventures, our desires, ourselves. The Caribbean is a place of great convergence; it mixes and uniforms diversities; it is a march of rhythm and style.

Those of us who have ventured off into writing should be in awe of the possibilities inherent in our tradition. Writing is behind the scenes; it is not like music and dance which engulf the masses. Poetry gets to the people in the form of lyrics within a bolero or a salsa tune. It is a valid form of expression, for it contains image and story line; it places old proverbs at the entrance of our contemporary ears. Poetry also lives in the oral tradition known as declamation. There is a warehouse of poems from the Spanish which are memorized and bellowed from the various corners of balconies and colors. The moon is in the tongue between the cheeks, the troubadours move between ceiba trees and plazas, their poetry full of the battles of love, romance, lost love, what to do within the pain of departure. Conversation, spontaneous chitchat constantly interchanging, is a poetry that arises all around us; it is poetry in flight, it is the magic of words bouncing off the pueblos, off the trees into the vines, it comes through the floor like an anaconda, it darts like lizards, it soars like garzas: this language of the Caribbean, this criollo incarnation. Full of passion and opinions, this is the language of our parents. We are the sons and daughters of campesinos, fishermen, farmers who cultivated café and tobacco, cutters of cane whose eyes contain the memory of ardent green vistas out of wooden windows within the hottest tropicality. They have pictures of the ocean tongues and the vibrant hugging of the coast upon a sofa within their retinas. They were spiritual mediums and santeros who worshiped natural forces tapped since time immemorial by African and indigenous societies.

As the children of these immigrants, we are at the center of a world debate; we can speak of the shift from agriculture to industry to technology and the toll it has taken upon the human equilibrium. Let us look at it with clear eyes in our trajectory from one language (Spanish) to another (English). What have we lost or gained? Claro, there is the beautiful lyricism, rhyming and blending of that great romance language, exemplified even in the reading of books on mechanical operations in which the words are still sonorous despite the subject. Is there an inner flower which passions its fragrance despite its being clothed in English words? I believe that this is happening in much U.S. Hispanic literature; the syntax of the English is being changed. This can be seen very prominently within the work of Alurista, a Chicano poet. In his recent work, the subject is the language itself; it is not that he merely plays with the language as some Anglo language experimenters do, for his poetry still contains social meanings directed towards personal and political change and awareness. We also find in the prose work of Rudolfo Anaya a natural Spanish pastoral style resounding through his English, a very relaxed, unharsh sentence. In both the English and the Spanish the poets and writers uphold a sensibility of Hispanitude.

We battle the sterility of Anglo culture, of television clichés; we labor at being ourselves in a land of weirdos, electric freaks who sit mesmerized in front of screens and buttons, only stopping to eat the farthest reaches of junk or to jerk off about some personal need to be understood, barking about having the freedom to do whatever nauseous things their lifestyles call for. You know that a pastime of the North American middle class now is to go out to fields and dress up in military fatigues and play war, shoot the commies or, better yet, shoot third-world guerrillas–shoot real guerrillas–and after that get back in the pickup and go down to Burger King and eat whatever that is. Meanwhile, the ozone layer is disappearing and, what's that song sung by Richie Havens "Here Comes the Sun"? Then they have that thing where they eat until they almost explode and then stick their fingers down their throat and vomit, solely to start the process again. It's an image culture: what you see is all there is. Jane Fonda in *Barbarella* was offering body; now that she has gained consciousness she is offering more body and even better build.

Did Richard Rodriguez fall down hard? Well there are those who jump quickly to attack him because he seemed to say the opposite of what was being fought for. Of course we must strive for an English that is standard and universal, a language that can be understood by as many people as possible, but why lose the Spanish in the process? We should change the English and give it spice, Hispanic mobility, all this can be done within the framework of understanding, whether the reader is Anglo or Latino.

U.S. Hispanics have not blended into Northern Americana because our roots stay fresh. Due to the close proximity of the Americans, rushes of tropical electricity keep coming up to inform the work and transform the North American literary landscape. The location and atmosphere of stories and poetry have been taken to places that until now North American authors were only able to write about from the position of tourists. The literature is full of border towns, farm workers, the lives of salsa musicians blowing through northern cities. The racial and cultural mixing of our cultures keeps us jumping through a huge spectrum of styles and philosophies. In terms of history, we can walk the planet with our genes, imagine ourselves in the Sevilla of the Arabs holding court with ibn 'Arabi and al-Ghazálí, quickly switch over to the halls of Tenochtitlán, then once again wake up in our contemporary reality dancing Yoruba choreography in some club in Manhattan near a subway train. You can change the content and mix into the infinite. Worlds exist simultaneously, flashes of scenarios, linguistic stereo; they conflict, they debate, Spanish and English constantly breaking into each other like ocean waves. Your head scatters with adverbs over the horizon.

All art forms borrow from each other for the purpose of enrichment. Architects can draw from ancient and colonial styles to arrive at their contemporary geometries—structures which improve human living. Musicians are constantly blending and mixing the rhythms of the earth; Caribbean music is like Andalucía and the Ivory Coast. In New York's Latin-Jazz fusion in the forties and fifties there are cuts where Tito Puente jams with Charlie Parker; this is like a toning of temperaments, or adjusting reality to get the most out of it. It seems to be the center of the musician to translate, rearrange, to give personal flavor to a variety of rhythms and melodies.

There are some words, so personal, so locked up in the oral and geographic area of a certain people that puns and stories have to be translated first into the standard language in order for them to be understood by speakers of the same language from another country, and passing them into another language is a labor of losing flavor, for there are things which remain within the mountains and can never be put into the textbook. If I said *un maflon* next to a Spaniard, he might look at me with a certain degree of curiosity and wonder what space I was coming from. Latinos speaking to each other have to constantly stop and review certain words. Sometimes when a word jumps over to the next country, it takes on an opposite meaning, or a word which you can yell in the plaza at the top of your voice, like *popusa* in El Salvador, moonlights as the private part of a woman in Guatemala. Anglos have difficulty grasping the variety of our world and have a tendency to slip us all under the same blanket in a careless act of generalizing, which upholds their manner: "Oh," they might say, "if you've read one Latino novel, you've read them all." In a system that works on quotas, this dispatches a lot of talented voices. Latin American writers publish with a lot more facility than U.S.-born Hispanics writing in English or Spanish. It is the habit of the establishment to enjoy things at a distance; package it with ease, throw the label "magic realism" on it—it's gotta be magic, unreal sells well as exotica. Now, we know who these writers are and I for one have great respect for them and their work, but because the Anglos work on quotas, the tremendous visibility of the Latin American writers obscures the chances for U.S. Hispanics of getting published by the same presses. It isn't the fault of these brilliant Latin American writers, but of the publicity machinery they get attached to. The society of the Americas is probably the most complex and diverse experiment in culture upon this earth and a full picture can only be obtained by allowing writers from many angles and countries to be exposed.

Unlike other groups who have had to erase their own cultural memories, Hispanics are moving forward, maintaining their own tradition and language. We will be the first group that does not melt; our ingredients are raw and the Anglo fire is not hot enough to dissolve them.

In the North of America it is a constant job just keeping ourselves from going looney-tunes, for this is a place where every stupidity is made available for the purpose of jamming the circuits. Explore, for example, the limited capacity of many in this electric culture to remember details of events: they are not able to tell stories. Computer screens have everybody dizzy, seeing dots in the air. Food preservatives are destroying taste buds. With all this going on, one must be on the watch: you gotta watch out that the next person doesn't jump and start acting out something he saw on television the previous night. It is the job of writers to perceive and explain the truth. To get to the essence of things in this society is a monumental task of awareness.

Celebrating Puerto Rican Style

For my children

Taking an airplane from one age to another was the highlight of my childhood.

You must get the picture of what it felt like to move, at five years old, from a small tropical village in Puerto Rico to New York City, the largest, most developed urban center on the planet. It was as if we penetrated another dimension. I remember my town, Aguas Buenas: small wooden homes with the touch of Spanish colonial, which in turn contained the Arabic influence of the Moorish occupation of Spain. The town's steep streets were surrounded by a green, lush flora from which descended the singing of the coquí, a unique Puerto Rican toad that permeates the island nights with its mating call.

The Puerto Rican migration of the late forties and early fifties was one of the great exoduses of recent times, emptying out much of the campesino population amid a collapse of the agricultural system, mainly sugar cane. The bulk of those immigrants arrived in the large northern cities of the U.S. mainland.

We are a people descended in part from the indigenous population that Columbus described as copper-skinned with straight jet black hair, living in oval-shaped villages of wooden homes that had palm-leaf rooftops. They had their own linguistic, religious and governmental systems until, the anthropologists tell us, this society was exterminated by the cruel policies of the Spaniards. In their quest for cheap labor, the Spaniards introduced Puerto Rico's African element, mostly Yorubas from that continent's west coast. And so the Indian, the Spaniard and the African are the ancestors of the Puerto Rican people – imparting a lasting flavor in language, music, food and spirituality which we describe as criollo.

On the island of Puerto Rico we never dream of a white Christmas or of a Santa Claus being guided through the clouds by Rudolph the Reindeer. On Christmas Day on our island it might be 87 degrees with the gentle East Trade Winds blowing. Islanders begin their festive spirit some three weeks before Christmas Day and go on for another two weeks after. It is as if Christ's radiance were descending upon the earth.

I remember Christmases as joyful and full of music. Aguinaldo, a form of Puerto Rican carol, jumps with the vitality of life, using drums, guitars and maracas. The songs speak of Jesus as if he were being born again that very moment when the voice and the heart administer the lyric. The songs glorify the Virgen María and her divine conception. They venerate the divine, and—as if on the same note—the joys of drinking rum and dancing, of flirting and falling in love, of piercing a hog with a spear and roasting it in the open air.

Jesus wants us to have a beautiful time, to dance the traditional mapayes, plenas and bombas as well as any boogaloo of invention on the day of his birth.

A most important feature of Christmas in the traditional towns of Puerto Rico is the asaltos or musical assaults. Each town has its own groups of singing bards who go on a musical rampages, stopping at the entrances of homes or directly below balconies, singing the famous Christmas jingles or improvising their own on the spot. At the end of their rendition it is the custom for members of the household to bestow gifts of food or drink as a sign of appreciation.

Coquito, a blend of coconut milk and rum, is a traditional Christmas drink that should be sipped sparingly, for it gives you the illusion that you can gulp it down like milk—a great way to end up falling down a mountain and finding yourself in a bushel of guayabas. The Puerto Rican pastel is another must around the holidays—grated plantain, pork meat, olives, garbanzos and hot peppers placed within a banana leaf and boiled. The aromas of this and other traditional dishes rise from Puerto Rico's towns on Christmas, waking the palates of the living and the dead.

In North America's cities, Christmas trees are purchased in lots set up under freeways. In Puerto Rico the tradition is different. The holiday of Los Tres Reyes Magos, the three wise kings, is celebrated on January 6th, and it is on that date that Puerto Rican children receive their gifts. But first they must prepare for them. Each must go out into the countryside with a box and gather grass. They then place the boxes under their beds, and it is there that they discover their gifts on the morning of January 6th. This grass under the bed is Puerto Rico's Christmas tree.

My island home is fighting for its cultural values and economic survival under the pressure of North American control. But at Christmastime Puerto Rico may have the upper hand. All airlines going into San Juan around the holidays are booked down to every seat. If you fly standby, rumor has it that sometimes you can get in but you can't get out.

Well, if that happens to you, take to the mountains of the interior, for those are the pictures sent by Christ from the heavens.

Feliz Navidad.

Salsa as a Cultural Root

Salsa literally means "sauce" in Spanish. It now identifies a dynamic-energetic driving Latin musical format which has its roots in Afro-Caribbean styles, most specific the Cuban Guaracha. The countries of Santo Domingo, Cuba and Puerto Rico have each contributed their local rhythms, but it was in the city of New York where the true synthesis manifested itself and Salsa was born.

The Puerto Rican community created a large audience which supported many local bands. Tropical music blasted out of the few Spanish radio stations. It was a habit of many of the deejays to throw on up-tempo mambos and merengues early in the morning, say about 6:30 or 7 AM to awake its Latin listeners with a boost and encourage them to go out and deal with freezing temperatures, snow and what-not as they scurried to work.

African drumming was preserved in the Caribbean. Drumming—originally a means of communication and religious invocation among peoples such as the Yorubas, which make up a great percentage of the Africans that were brought to the Caribbean—remains till this day very authentic and similar to its African counterpart. In Cuba, for instance, religious chants are still sung in original African languages such as Congolese and Arare. A unique African-derived language, Ñañíco, persists in many Cuban santería cults.

Afro-Cuban religious rhythms developed into the popular rumba which combined drumming and song, beautiful lyricism accompanying polyrhythms, songs that were rendered in Spanish with the addition of African words. The songs spoke of love, the daily life of the Cubans. Many of the songs reached high philosophical levels, as can be appreciated in the tunes written by the blind Cuban tres player Arsenio Rodriguez, it was a people's poetry which blasted out of the side streets of Habana, finally entering the salons of society. Spanish melodies weaved through the African beat.

Out of the rumba many other forms developed, the guaguancó, the cha-cha-chá. These rhythms were made popular in the States by musicians such as Tito Rodriguez, Mongo Santamaria and Tito Puente. Another Cuban rhythm, the Mambo, which means "female priestess" in Santeria, took hold in New York during the mid-fifties. The Palladium, a popular club on New York's 53rd Street, was the gathering place of dancers. It was located around the corner from Birdland, a jazz club which featured the exponents of bebop. Jazz and Latin musicians went back and forth from each other's rhythms, creating a very special blend of Latin Jazz. Dizzy Gillespie was at the forefront of this development. Through his relationship with Chano Pozo he made Afro-Cuban drumming and chants a part of his music and opened the way for further innovation.

The North American public first got a glimpse of Latin rhythms on the "I Love Lucy Show," where her husband Ricky Ricardo featured his own band and swayed into Anglo ears such words as *Babalu Aye*, which is Yoruba in origin. All of these musical events paved the way for the arrival of the music which we now know as Salsa.

The Puerto Rican community had been developing since the twenties. At first many merchant seamen settled their families along the waterfront in Brooklyn. This area, known as Williamsburg, has in recent years been renamed Los Sures by its Puerto Rican residents.

East Harlem was also developing as a Puerto Rican enclave. In the forties it was populated by Spaniards, Cubans and the lingering German families. Its Third Avenue featured cigar-making workshops manned by Spaniards and Cubans. It was not long before it was overwhelmed by Puerto Ricans, changing for good the flavor and feeling of the area. The smell of fried plantains and red beans sailed through the bricks. Recently arrived señoritas could be seen getting out of cars just arriving from New York's La Guardia Airport with gardenias still freshly posed in their waving black hair. The moon walking as a glow through the fire escapes of the tenements.

As the Latin community solidified in the city, so did the demand for Latin entertainment and products. Bodegas (corner grocery stores) sprouted up featuring tropical produce, good strong coffee–which Puerto Ricans and Cubans always demand–and an assortment of other paraphernalia, such as candles and herbal rubbing alcohols to deal with physical and spiritual ailments. Bodegas transplanted Caribbean spices into the monstrous belly of New York.

Theaters such as the Puerto Rico in the Bronx, the Cosmo in the heart of Spanish Harlem and the Jefferson on Manhattan's Lower East Side featured Mexican films with such stars as Jorge Negrete, Miguel Aceve Mejias and the actor-comedian Cantinflas. After the films it was showtime: a spotlight appeared on the red curtain and the emcee came out of a slice doing a flurry of jokes which led into the acts – dancers, magical acts, singers such as the Chilean Lucho Gatica, trios like Los Condes and some of the big Latin orchestras which were developing in New York's Latin dance halls. Children ran up and down the aisles, a murmur was constantly coming from the audience, no one complained or expected the place to be in absolute silence like a European opera house.

Second-generation Puerto Rican musicians kept the city hot with their interpretations of Caribbean rhythms, many doing the Cuban tunes of the forties and fifties with only slight changes in the structures. Salsa music has an undercurrent rhythmic law known as the clave, which is 1-2 (pause) 1-2-3. This rhythm should be the undertow of any Latin tune, be it a guaracha, a mambo or a guaguancó; musicians merely speed it up or slow it down, melodies decorate above or below it, or simultaneously along with it. As the rhythm and melody churns, it gives the sensation of a kaleidoscope, a huge mandala turning. This facilitates the dancers, who spin, holding hands, occasionally coming apart to administer backward and forward motions. The Yorubas are the great choreographers of Africa, the Latin dance steps still exhibit their great knowledge of rhythmic patterns. Present also in Latin dance is the flamenco of the Spaniards or, more accurately, of the Gypsies. It must also be related to Arabian choreography for much of Spanish style derives its energy and flavor from that Muslim culture, which made itself at home on their soil for close to 800 years. Latin music, like Latin dance, follows a pattern: it starts suave; the introduction, all the instruments do not come in at once; everything depends on the arrangement; the singer comes in and plants his theme, accompanied by a chorus which jumps in right after him, emphasizing the main poetic idea of the song; the orchestra grows towards an area where individual instruments can take a solo if it is in the calling; once this is over, they gather back on to a plateau, which is similar to the intro; the music gathers momentum and rises to a takeoff area where they all accelerate together. This last is the area of frenzy and possession which is a feature of both African and Arabian music. The dancers should also be following the vibrations and should be on the verge of personal disappearance. Latin dance is as close as one can come to the whirling of the dervishes, the renowned mystics of Islam.

New York City Latin music also went through a period which was labeled the Latin Bugalú. This occurred around the mid-sixties and lasted a few years. The close proximity of the Afro-American community to the Puerto Rican community created a merger. English lyrics with a soul orientation were added to the Latin beat, and young city Latinos danced the boogaloo to the Latin soul beat. Willie Colon was an early exponent of this tendency, though he soon abandoned it to get back on track, going back to Jíbaro (Puerto Rican mountain) roots and even Brazilian samba. The Latin Bugalú was a big craze and many bands heeded the calling, providing a string of hits. The traditional Latin bands had to jump on the bandwagon or get no gigs and little air-play. Johnny Colon's "Boogaloo Blues" can be pinpointed as the matrix number. Though the Spanish-language radio stations boycotted this new music, the Latin Bugalu found an outlet on the late night English-speaking radio shows of Dick Ricardo Sugar, an old man who looked like an insurance salesman, and Symphony Sid. Symphony Sid had his start a generation earlier featuring jazz. As Latin music became popular, he began to change his format, at first throwing in a few Latin tunes, later going to half and half, till Latin became the better part of his show. The new progressive and improvisational Latin of Eddie and Charlie Palmieri, Tito Puente, Machito, Mongo Santamaria, Johnny Pacheco, to mention a few, made their way out of these two late-night FM radio shows. Symphony Sid played both the traditional Spanish lyric Latin and the new Latin Bugalú. Till this day there is a controversy as to the musical worth of the Latin Bugalú period in New York. The clave, the rhythmic law of Afro-Cuban music, was sometimes abandoned. English lyrics replaced the flavorful and expressive Spanish of Cuba, Puerto Rico and Santo Domingo. You couldn't sing about sugar cane, mangoes, pineapples, red beans, magical herbs like Gerba Buena, Ruta, Albaca— all these themes and contents were lost, but only for that while, for both the Latin audience and the musicians demanded a return to the roots, and in the long run the rhythms of the Caribbean have survived. It only demonstrated the ability of the criollo peoples of the islands to synthesize new systems, to incorporate them in their frames and maintain their own identity.

What is very important to note is that the Latin Bugalu was a special feature of the New York City Puerto Rican (Nuyorican) experience. As working-class peoples and descendants of Africans, Taino Indians and Spaniards from Andalusia – that area of Iberia which most absorbed Arabian and Gypsy cultures – they were more than qualified to make this amalgamation. It is for this reason that the popularity of Salsa music is so widespread: it contains something for everybody. Musicians such as Israel "Cachao" Lopez from Cuba and New York Puerto Rican pianist Eddie Palmieri incorporate elements of European classical music into their performances, sometimes in the middle of exciting guarachas. Other times they open with Vivaldi or Ravel movements and sustain it with cellos and violins, so that their sound is indistinguishable from, let's say, the Boston Symphony Orchestra doing similar interpretations of these masters.

Even the popular music of the fifties, known as duwop, was incorporated into the music during the Latin Bugalú era of New York. Duwop sprang out of Black neighborhoods in Philadelphia and New York, and became the sound of the North American working class. It went from coast to coast, entering Puerto Rican, Chicano and Italian neighborhoods, providing a Romantic landscape for many teenage lovers. The Spanials, The Harptones, The Crows were among the first groups to popularize this music that was once performed on street corners and in tenement hallways. The Crest of "Sixteen Candles" fame hailed from the Lower East Side of Manhattan and were composed of Blacks, Italians and Puerto Ricans. Brooklyn Italians demonstrated their ability at the art of a cappella, perhaps an extension of the popular love songs of Italy coming across the Atlantic to merge with the Black duwop soul. Listen to the Italian group The Duprees in such hits as "Have You Heard" to feel their particularly velvety celestial harmony. Within the early Salsa sound in New York, Joe Bataan and Rafi Pagan would come in sometimes after a sweaty mambo and mellow the place out with soulful duwop renditions of "If This World Were Mine" and "I Want To Make It with You."

As can be seen, heard and felt, Salsa, which originally identified the red tomato saw poured into beans, is an extension of the criollo culture of the Americas, especially as it manifests itself in the area of the Caribbean. This experiment in racial and spiritual mixing, this hodge-podge of humanity was well described by the Mexican scholar José Vasconcelos as the Cosmic Race. Brazil and Puerto Rico are the two countries where the racial and cultural merge are the most replete.

One needs solely to study the music, the faces and the colors to appreciate this great advance in living. It should also serve as an education for the North, as an example that it might follow, abandoning its bigotry and fears. It should let itself go and melt into the total America. Truly, we will be the New World.

Foreword*

These are the ages of poems, of poems that rapid through the skull and spit fire through doorway mouth like waterfalls the airs set full with adventure, a telling, a walking of the words. Contemporary with such swiftness as to have current events, the art itself is later and hangs out of the necessities of tribal communication. It is still the song of those who left for Aztlán, whether Aztlán is the North and thus the Bay Bridge or a star in the Andromeda constellation or a sensation in the heart. The two hearts that grew the pens in Spanish plumes to write brief poetic notes are bound together through spiritbone and being mestizo explore inner angles of immense collections, sometimes cosmic in frame but never losing family. Perhaps, what the great Spanish poet Lorca was all about, a kind of folkloric experimentation, Campesino AvantGarde, corn with electricity. Chicano poetry always brings you home, no matter where it goes; following the biological makeup of our inner bodies, or speculating on lost Mexican traditions such as in the poem by Juan Felipe where he suddenly jumps from the English and uses the words *de aquéllas*. Who in English-speaking America would know what *de aquéllas* means, this flavorful and multi-meaningful Chicano expression used to denote exhilaration or the overabundance of a good thing? This is an important element of Hispanic North American poetry. The old Spanish battles with the Anglo occupation of the mind, it also incorporates that inner Hispanic humor and twist of being into the English, giving the English a dance on the edges. What really dashes out of these small manifestations is the emotions that come to soothe you no matter how they decorate it, these are tidbits of Juan and Margarita, a poetry of struggle and love, of family and community, a search for personal and international justice, poetic justice. Served here are these bronze hors d'oeuvres. Enjoy. Buen Provecho.

---

*The pieces that follow are introductions to *Facegames*, a book of poems by Juan Felipe Herrera and to *A Night in Tunisia*, his joint venture with his wife, Margarita Lunas Robles – they gathered their bones and crumbled them into flowers.

Entreversión

Poetry is the flowers which grow out of experience, after turmoil comes contemplation: mother-of-pearl boats on the Pacific. It is peaceful thought that rhythmically dances with and explains, reacts to, reality. Music is a biological treatment upon the nerves totally destroying us. Poetry enters through reason and makes us disappear; the heavens could be similar, but everyone uses different transportation.

With Juan Felipe Herrera we could say that his mind is at his ankles, in his belly or somehow ahead of you in the room you are about to enter. In the person and in the poetry the entity knows no limitations — his light zooms down on Mexico City, San Diego, the Mission District of San Francisco, Cactus; it swings from Cactus into the imagery of the 1950s. We get views of small California towns and pre-urban characters who saw the construction trucks en route towards the city carrying the materials to build skyscrapers.

The mark of a great poem is the administration of balance, between action and meditation, the earthly and celestial, the imaginative life flirting with the practical. Within Juan Felipe's poetry we find this quality present as if organically, it is there without the need of strenuous thought to mold it.

Think of the crossroads he is suspended in: linguistically, Spanish and English. Through the Spanish he is connected to the great poetic pulse of Spain and Latin America, to the singers of Boleros and cultivators of El Cuento. His mind is constantly translating back and forth between two world languages, and we are all the more enriched by his method of synthesis. The Spanish of the Americas unifies diversities. It has been infused with indigenous and African vocabularies. As such, it is the language of evolution, it secretly contains old Arabian tales and ancient native mythological flashbacks — Herrera is drippling all this through the tongue of Milton and Shakespeare. But, his English is not English. He might not be able to go to Margaret Thatcher's house with his Hispanectical hybrid verses. But, neither would Thatcher be able to visit his adobe, making the vacuum for her much greater 'cause there's a mean chili at Juan Felipe's place that could stretch your tongue beyond the confines of your cheek.

His poetry expands without missing the minute, he takes local issues into the stars, he listens to the suggestion made by neighborhood folklore and takes it beyond the horizon. I was going to say *minuet* instead of *minute* because it is also a dance of organized flurries. Look at that *or* quickly followed by another *or* to go on to *ganized*: he breaks the language down in that manner, occasionally exploding into sculpture.

He is a learned poet mixing reality to the explosions of language sound. He is interested in both the shape and meaning of his deliveries, he filters all global cultures through his classical seashell. History and politics weave through the poetry in nondogmatic forms. Study how he could mix the qualities of an essay into a lyric. He sets the issue of politics versus art for us into perspective; he is looking for a liberation that is much more than just physical rupture, he unhinges our minds from colonialisms and imperialisms whether personal or governmental with the intonations of his words. He knows that the space of nature will blast through all the polemics—he seems to know what people mean even when they themselves don't know what they are saying.

Juan Felipe Herrera is as close as we come to a total expression mechanism. His senses are not just multicultural; they are coming at us through a variety of artistic forms. He is a writer, poet, musician and actor; he could make you the rail carrying a train-shaped blues guitar. He lives on the wires connecting all forms, and readers of this book are only getting a glimpse of what he is doing—you must imagine the gestures, the pantomime, the street talker, the singer. His inventive somersaults are always packed with a parade of information that helps us live the now. When he writes about events that have occurred, they seem to be following him; that is because he knows the symbols and is not fooled by anything, not stuck on trivial facts. His poetry reveals to us and leaves us naked in that mirror. Because it is a game that the Gods are playing.

Taos: The Poetry Bout
Codrescu vs. Cruz

In Puerto Rico as well as Brazil there is a form known as Controversia in which two singing bards go into combat, throwing poetic jingles at each other. On the island of Puerto Rico it is carried out in the ten-line Spanish décima, accompanied by musicians playing guitars and gourds. The musicians, synchronized superbly with the poets, know exactly when to come in – so a poet singer better take care of his business within the allotted time. Infringement into the musical portion is already a sign of weakness and reason enough for defeat.

The idea is to insult and diminish your opponent, to list his bad qualities and exalt your superiority. Since these songs are improvised, many immediate things come into the jingles. Like the way one of the bards finds the other one dressed – if he is wearing a hat too big or a pair of pants hanging too high that becomes part of the ammunition. One of the singers might shoot:

If you cannot properly attire
yourself
How could you stand there
and sing
Go back home and start
all over again

The other poet might retort:
I'd rather have material
missing on my pants
Than to have it missing
from my brain
Besides look at your shoes
Perhaps it is your habit
to step on dog doo

The battle would go on until one of the singers runs out of décimas and the other tops him off.

The poetic bout which Codrescu and I participated in had none of these strict laws of meter. It went 9 rounds, each of which consisted

104

of one poem read aloud from text. Only the last round was improvised, based upon a theme selected from a jar. We could say that these poetic bouts rely heavily on the mood of the audience and the judges. An audience might be in a social-realist mood, looking to see how the poet relates to social issues, how he or she uses craft to support political struggles. Or the audience might be into surrealism, or concerned with language poetry, who knows exactly what that is. In Taos we were lucky in that the audience was not particularly dedicated to any poetic school; it was all delivery and drama, making poetry the winner. It became a heightened reading, with the both of us cutting our lines with nuclear razors, sometimes in Spanish and sometimes in Roumanian and always with an accent.

My own accent out of the Spanish has its moods. It starts leaning toward Spanish at night. There are conscious moments when I try to charge into the English like Sir Lancelot and fill all the curves of its letters, take those syllables with coconut oil. When I was in Puerto Rico, I was surrounded by Spanish. Now that I am back in the U.S. of A. I am engulfed by English, so my Spanish stands up inside; phrases sail across in slow motion. Every time I hear English I give myself an immediate translation into Spanish. An accent is the lingering memory of the tongue true to its first formations, something that pulls back through the saliva to original utterances. Andrei Codrescu has an accent that's like a three-piece suit. His English is almost Roumanian. It is that Eastern European accent à la exaggerated Dracula. I threw a poem in Spanish and Codrescu threw a poem in Roumanian, the rest were in an English that tilted.

Taos has an Ibero-Indian flavor, making it feel Latin American. With a sensational landscape that makes one's eyes go out for miles like a glide through the clouds, to see the Rio Grande Gorge – an immense opening in the mountains – is to come close to bliss. It was through this beautiful countryside that Andrei and I took off to prepare for our bout that evening. We crisscrossed roads that looked like lines disappearing into the horizon, finally coming to Ojo Caliente, where we dove into hot mineral baths full of rancheros with bellies full of Corona. They spoke to each other in Spanish so I joined them in chitchat while we soaked in water so hot it gave you immediate second thoughts.

After the pool we were wrapped with green blankets like some vegetable and laid out to dry. As I tried to put my bones back together from the meltdown, I thought of strategy for the evening reading. I had selected some poems but didn't know the order in which I would read them. I wanted to counter the poems that Codrescu read, so I would wait to hear the content, temperament, style of his poems and read something which would reflect an opposite area of concern. If he read a tragic or a philosophical poem I would resort to humor, or to counter metaphysics I would read a poem with a story line, where the simplicity of the events would add up to a similar inquiry. In other words, if he threw a left I would throw a right. I had to be aware of over-reading, of presenting poems that were too long and hermetic and possibly hard to follow. I had uppercuts in the form of haikus and sonnets, but when to throw those punches would be determined by Codrescu's maneuverings. The gladiator spirit exists in poetry at many levels so why not focus it with a poetry reading bout? Maybe in the future they could put some spice in it by having poets of differing schools read next to each other, e.g., feminist poets with anti-feminist poets. After all, it is a circus.

The moment of the bout, Andrei and I went up on stage as reserved as possible, with a bottle of Jack Daniels and smirks on our faces. The audience cheered and booed. According to Lewis MacAdams, who made twenty dollars on a bet, some money was being exchanged on the floor, perhaps as much as eighty dollars. According to the *Taos News* there were some 500 people in the audience.

When I first heard of the Poetry Bout I immediately thought: only in North America could poets engage in such leisurely activity. Most world poets are involved in questions of national identity and liberation. The act of writing could be deadly in most Hispanic countries. Writing must be specific to meaning to explore the center of spiritual and political existence. It is a personal and collective healing process. It is to fight oppression—whether it be of a family or governmental nature—that we express ourselves. Everything I do in poetry must have a meaning beyond itself that is the center of metaphor. In North American society the poet is isolated from the masses, making him a loner. Not so in the Hispanic culture. Many of the poems of Federico García Lorca are now the popular songs of Spain. The same is the case throughout the Americas. To create is to find yourself in others. That is why we are involved in language, which is the height of communication.

The public poetry reading is the great forum of mental and emotional meaning coming at us orally. It is the least expensive form of entertainment in this land of electric gadgetry. To keep that spirit up is why I entered the ring at the Taos Poetry Circus. These debates between poets can only sharpen the poetic presentation, and it must be done with a great sense of humor. So gua-gua-gua I say to my possible opponent next year. She or he better bring rhythm, content and flavor, for I am sharpening the nails of my rooster, and I don't care where their content is from, for I am a Caribbean frog—and those jump every-which-a-way.

Light-Mambo and Photography

With the photography of Adal Maldonado we'd have to reverse the old Chinese saying that "One picture is worth a thousand words." With his style it would be best to say that a single word can become a million pictures. His photographic art is by now known on both coasts of the United States, in Europe where he has had shows and certainly in his native Puerto Rico where he has become the photographer of show business. Those portraits, mainly of Salsa artists, have become a giant of a photographic book entitled *Mango Mambo*, published by his own Old San Juan Studio: Ilustres Studios.

The prologue by Edgardo Rodriguez Julia pieces together what the age of photography has meant nationally (Puerto Rico) and internationally, that visual mummification holding the youth which vanishes from our grasp. The commentary of Julia, who is both novelist and art and social critic, makes us aware of the inner meaning of the portraits, of the faces which bring to us orchestral sounds and memories of where we were when that hit came out. He brings them into focus with personal and national anecdotes. Julia is intuitively aware of Adal's photographic philosophy. The artist who takes the pictures neither gives or takes anything from his posing subjects (victims). He lets them be; he "surprises" them in their aware unawareness, saturated in the glory of their fame.

With the notorious precipitation habit that Aguas Buenas enjoys or puts up with, with that natural ability of having no choice, I am sure that Edgardo Rodriguez Julia, who is rumored to be partially from here, had enough fecundity of eye to perceive in the portrait of Rafael Ithier, the director of El Gran Combo, that he was "more serious than a penny's worth of bread." It could be that same fecundity which contributes to the editorial greatness of his observations of the observations of Adal's camera. He must know quite well that if it is not raining, it's because it's going to rain.

The afterword is by none other than Tite Curet Alonso, Salsa's great composer of songs. He is to Salsa what Bob Dylan was to rock music in its heyday. The book is really a survey of contemporary Caribbean music. It includes shots of Tito Puente, Eddie Palmieri, Ray Barretto, Mario Bauza and the late Charlie Palmieri. He sees the totality of our

108

musical expression and does not just stick to rhythmic music but also features such popular singers as Carmita Jimenez, a woman who becomes the boleros that she sings, each lyric sending her into sensual and sad contortions. Lucecita Benítez he has posed in front of a mirror, and we get her reflection and then off to the side about ten percent of her real face, with one of the greatest noses ever seen. To finish the picture off, Antonio Martorell has done her profile in red lipstick. She is wearing a gala white gown with diamonds on the shoulders; it is of such lustful quality that we can almost smell the lipstick and perfume.

Adal knows intimately the music of each artist. He is from Utuado, Puerto Rico, a town that is decorated by the greatest of tropical scenery as you enter it, complete with a river that divides into two and disappears into the basement of a mountain. He also grew up in New York and came of age within its Latin music dance halls. He has Paquito D'Rivera holding what looks like a mahogany clarinet and a Panama hat hanging on his right knee, reminding me of celestial wind swooping through plantains and coasts where history made the music of various continents merge. The shot of Papo Lucca, the piano player and former musical director of La Sonora Ponceña, makes him feel as if he was in motion through the sky. Tito Puente is holding his two timbal sticks and has undone his tie, as if he had just finished a jam in which he hailed upon the timbal skins like tropical rains which sometimes do not leave any room between drops. When we flip the page we get a shot of Tito's back and once again the two timbal sticks being held by his palms. Puente's musical variety required two angles for his polyrhythmical self.

The shot of Daniel Santos is also two pictures, this time small photos one next to the other. Daniel Santos, Puerto Rico's wandering singing bard, has created a big following in neighboring Latin American countries, where he has also resided for periods of his life, sometimes not in very good standing with the authorities. He is a rebel and he lives his songs of erotic adventure and debauchery. In both frames he is holding a cigarette, one shows him smiling, in the other he is dead serious. Eddie Palmieri, the 20th portrait of the book, gives us a pair of glazed eyes, making the pianist look like he made contact with Vivaldi or the mother of pianos. *Piano* is that Italian word which resides within the Spanish. The Palmieris are Puerto Ricans with a dose of Italian blood. Joe Cuba [portrait 21] looks like a buccaneer, the top part of his head is missing, but that is rumored to be a toupee.

Luis "Perico" Ortiz is captured by Adal playing his trumpet into the sky, perhaps at passing birds. A second picture of Perico is more of his trumpet, for his face is hidden by the brilliant brass mouth of his trumpet, which is full of images which cannot be made out. Yomo Toro, who is not Japanese despite the name, is hugging his cuatro guitar to his chest, wearing a white hat and a flowered shirt, the kind that New York City Puerto Ricans used to identify with recent arrivals from the island. Adal caught the moment when Yomo was laughing hysterical, his face all blossomed out, making Yomo with his tremendous round body gleam like a Buddha.

Rafael Cepeda Atiles is an image to behold. He is Puerto Rico's grandfather of the Bomba. The Bomba is one of our African-derived national rhythms and song styles. He is sporting an all-white suit complete with vest, and crowning his head is a white Panama hat. Within his hands he is carrying a cane made of dark wood. Is he not honor being carried by garzas back to Africa within that singular glance of the lens?

In Ruth Fernandez we have a different kind of ritual. Both her hands are risen as if she is about to receive the holy spirit within a Pentecostal storefront church. Her dress is a gown of sequins, each shining as if electric.

Millie and Jocelyn Quesada, the dynamic head of the Nuyodominican group known as Millie y Los Vecinos, are caught in all their gusto as they lean one upon the other. They exhibit so much joie de vivre without the need of psychotherapy that it could just be the presence of the Antilles, its flavors and rhythms, within their hearts. Their shapes, their aerobics is the merengue.

Ednita Nazario, another of the pop singers, is coming out of a black shadow which is also her dress. She is holding her throat with both her hands as if a million desires and promises of love were erupting out of her in the form of romantic ballads. Her head is thrown back, giving a prominence to her lips, and if she were a landing field I'd manufacture airplanes made out of tongues.

Adal's photograph of the singer Nydia Caro is pure dream. She is the principle of womanhood, serene and on fire at the same time. Her eyes are shut and her head is thrown back slightly. Her shoulders are exposed, perfect balances, and her hands are placed upon her waist as if wings. She is in a shining dress of silver. It is a tribute to Adal's sense of composition, to his photographic editing, to his feel for the limitations and proper exposure of a good presence that he stopped at the waist and didn't give us a full body picture which would have brought us to the gates of paradise and destroyed the aesthetic pleasure of suggestion. As Tite Curet Alonso points out in the afterword, this is a book "conceived with discernment and a watchful eye, especially designed to be a proper frame for the details that are presented."

Taking pictures of the farandula is just one dimension of Adal Maldonado's photographic character. He is also a composer of collages, setting up arrangements that come from some subreality of his mind. In this respect, when he functions as an artist, he is unsatisfied with the visual world, he does not want to be a mere documenter of the material of appearance. He plays with the laws of logic and wakes us up to swing on the branches of our minds, which we only grasp in dreams. In these photos we discover faces which are appearing out of walls without bodies, parts of the anatomy gone into mirrors or chairs. In a photo entitled "Sitio de Debate" (Point of Debate) we get a sharp view of the dashboard of a car and its rearview mirror. But look close—the mirror does not reflect the rear but is a clear view of what is in front of the car—a man walking by, that part of his body which enters the rearview mirror is invisible. That was all unexpected, so you wonder What else can be out there? Adal is constantly at war with our senses, using these details as weapons. It is as if he is a photographer of the spirit world, his medium the camera. Each photo is actually a multilayered short story. There are pictures within pictures, like the patterns in the *Arabian Nights*, the Bible and other Middle Eastern narratives. His photos are collisions of metaphors, they are essays presented in the form of images. Within that photographic journey the vision fits their visitations to his mind; he needs no Kirlian methods of photography to see the electromagnetic fields that are out there dancing Mambo all around the carcasses, he sees them in plena light. Equipment then must obey his commands. It is a technological skill which he marries to fertile soil, red soil which can grow new varieties of mango, perhaps mango mixed with guanabana, Mangoguana, a new fruit on the market, a new taste for your tongue. Adal works light the way Rembrandt worked light, sky coming out of edges. If we claim that Rembrandt worked his light within a much slower method because of the age he lived in and the different medium, we are wrong, they both got it in a flash. Rembrandt went for his paintbrush, Adal for his camera equipment. Flash on Flash. What is it that tells us we have captured something perfectly, accurately, at its best moment of reproduction, which no one else can equal, which no one else can find even if they had the same materials at hand, be it poem, painting or photo? Could it be in Adal's case the first light he saw coming down from the mountains of Utuado, that town full of indigenous structures, that aboriginal air of our twilight depositing itself within his retina?

The Low Writings

Who first in the human planet invented the wheel, its use as transport. Now see it, someone caressing a mountain watching rocks and pebbles rolling, coming to a stop in front of their toes. Just picture, gee, if we were ants clinging, or something more minute, unnamed creatures of the tropical berserk, an orange pinhead moving with eight legs, the ancients must have said how quickly this carries it through the terrain. Now the first hatchback could have been inside rocks, or in the dream to be a pelota flying through a Taino park, send a message which travels distance and I can catch it with my fingers.

Out here puffing, jamming, moving down boulevard, deep into the industry of tires, red wheels, blue tires, metal sunk low around it, like a closed eye or a blink, constructions floating, homemade interiors, Roman Chariots dodging, trunks full of batteries. In Peru the llama was freight carrier over through mountains, paths whose history they were starting; for gasoline they gave them chicha and coca leaves, zoom through streams, atop where it's cold down to the hot flatlands, edges of towns where they traded woven blankets and disappeared into the clouds. And that petrol took them through sky tree branches, the llama white and bushy, serene, a caravan of miniature camels.

When I am in this room that flies it is as if I invented rubber. Like San Jose low rider's interiors, fluffy sit back, unwind, tattoo on left hand, near the big thumb a cross with four sticks flying, emphasizing its radiance, further up the arm skeletons, fat blue lines, Huichol designs on the copper flesh, the arm of the daddio on the automatic stick. A beautiful metal box which many call home. It doesn't matter if the manufacturer was Ford or General Motors, their executives in the suburbs of Detroit watching home movies, vacationing in weird Timbuktus, when the metal is yours you put your mark on it. Buying something is only the first step, what you do to it is your name, your history of angles, your exaggeration, your mad paint for the grand scope of humanity, the urbanites will see them like butterflies with transmissions. Take it to Mexico and get a round figure, to the maniacs of Tijuana, who break it down to slices, throw it back together, slice it up again.

Once a circus caravan of riders from Watsonville took twenty cars down, puffing and flying and bouncing all the way; only stopped twice by Highway Patrol, but they looked so loony that the officers, perhaps behind a beer or two, let them go, saying this can't be real, plus they were clean as a Mormon in Salt Lake City, license and registrations, and hydraulics well hidden.

Zoom, all en route towards TJ to get their interiors laid out, they know who to see, one tall Tony, another guy called Gordo, talk right adjust your price, Tigar, Zeebra, velvet, polka dots, colors your dream, shit never heard of, tugged in tight, last you a century, you go before your car will, blazing stuff, shag rug pink running across dashboard.

Twenty cars rolling, eating the road from here to Tijuana, from here to Tia Juana, music from The Pioneers. All the mozos, some with mozas, sporting lumberjack shirts, leaning, brown hands, the tattoo cross where Christ was tortured, on the steering wheel cutting edges, a mosaic of tongues rattling, can we say unidentified flying objects, private discos, patterns, a piece here and a piece there, if that don't work enter the garage of spare parts.

Mission Street is El Camino Real, is the old road of Christianity. If you start riding from 24th you could go in a straight line all the way to the gates of gold. From path to road from road to street to avenue from avenue to boulevard from boulevard to airport from airport continue to space station, looking for those white cristals.* Don't kid yourself, the Northern proposition has always been vertical, an uptown kind of motion, towards the mechanics who laid out your interior, how real is the Camino, El Camino Irreal where car junkies glide into the southern and northern lights.

The scene on the road must be here comes Ali Baba and his twenty machines, going South to get to their North. But wait, how long will this oil supply last, 2050, you cannot replace it like coffee or tobacco. Columbian oil gives its own seeds, but the blood of the earth, once it's taken out, leaves space. Do you figure they will be able to equip motors with new gadgets that will allow them to digest an alternate source of energy? Si no, se acabo la Honda. The whole landscape will be full of rust, only the low riders' pleasure boats will be assigned to museums. Tony blows/ And my hand against the dashboard, in my studio roving, dazzling right below the mini charro hat swinging from the rearview mirror, with its embroidery in gold and silver, gold rings you bunch of susus, exhibit relaxation, the State of California made roads for us, the princes in shiny cabins.

Who invented wheels, invented roads, but movement, which is before avenues, before circles, invented itself, it made enough of itself to be available to all, to be interpreted according to each. It's like you enter and perform, like the full fleet of twenty cars riding towards TJ will each have its own coat, their common language is their closeness to the ground, they want to kiss the earth, they want to penetrate the many disguises of their mama land. Have we been in touch with you, are we rubbing you right, to be on this road, is this the way we say love, dangling from a window, driving Smokey Robinson and the Miracles, Ooooo Baby Baby Oooooo Baby baby, green light go, stop light red stop, yellow light put your feet down tight. In the hot rod land what can we do with our hands but attack the steel, mold it, make it unique, each will be different for the same purpose.

Hector blows: When my cacharro goes down, there's not even room to stick a nickel in at the bottom. The steering wheel is the handle of measurement: skinny ones, made of silver chains, prisoner chains, industrial chains, smoking chains, the smaller steering wheels allow for quick jerky precise turns, tricks that only roadrunner could perform, beep beep. Make room for the modern car yachts of the Watsonville Road Kings, monarchs of the boulevards, never bored always going somewhere, now en route south, towards the land of the articulate mechanics, who work with their eyes closed and create, short of putting a toilet in the back. A style of craftsmanship, concentration, it features remnants of a classical point of view, the car is the living room, like Gothic mixed with Toltecas, my space to freak you out. Come delight in my red peach-fuzz sofas, enjoy the stereo sound from my Pioneer speakers, picture the chrome hanging like a painting in a gallery, car club emblems showing through the back windows: Watsonville Road Kings, jumping and moving, cleaning the surface, when the gasoline stops pumping the vehicles will run on perfume and music.

*The word *cristals* can only be the word *crystals:* a clear, transparent mineral or glass resembling ice, or the transparent form of crystallized quartz. If we were hearing the word instead of seeing it in print, we would have no problem with the meaning. *Cristal* in Spanish means "glass," with an *s* it could go on to imply glassy or shiny. In the story it refers to Aztlán which is supposed to be a star in the Andromeda constellation but I don't believe this at all, do you?

A good friend of mine, Andres Segura from Mexico City, was the deer dancer for many years with El Ballet Folklórico and is also versed in Nahuatl perspectives – not as a student but as an heir to the tradition. He dispensed this information on the word *Aztlán:* it signifies "White Gauze" – what the Chicanos call the mythical land of the Aztecas. He goes on further to say it is actually this extremely brightly lit white speckling stretch of stars which are the gateway to God's house or heaven, home of the Creator, and he specified that it was also a name given to one star in Andromeda and that to them North didn't mean yonder horizontally but yonder vertically. Thus, looking for white crystals means looking for your salvation, for your orientation, for accuracy, agility. I prefer that you change it to the proper spelling – crystals – since it will bring more people on board.

Don Arturo: A Story of Migration

Don Arturo has never been on an airplane. When he came from Cuba he took a boat; it was 1926. He had met a minister's wife in Habana, and she invited him to come and join her husband's touring musical Christian band in the States. Don Arturo thought about it for a few days.

He worked as an errand boy at the Habana Opera House; he had met Caruso and brought him coffee. He was around classical music in a tropical setting.

His family hailed from Valencia, Spain. His father played guitar, and Don Arturo picked it up like water down a dry throat. His brothers and sisters numbered eight, and he was the oldest. He helped raise them, and they had no money but they had a farm. They made food stretch like Jesus said to do.

Cuba was in turmoil and the economy was like a special delivery from the devil. The Guajiros rebelled, coming down the mountains, angry like fighting roosters. He saw men shoot men with guns in the head; they fell down like sacks of rice.

When he was 18 he left the countryside to go to Habana to pursue being a priest. The priests in Cuba did what they wanted, including making love to the young women. Yes, my dear, confess your sins; they brought down skirts like peeling bananas. He got along with God but not with the Church. When he couldn't take it any more, he left for the guitar and learned how to play the harmonica.

He jumped into Habana nightlife like a bee into a flower. The Opera House was full of stars, and he mingled and got advice from them. He saw costumes, people rehearsing, and all kinds of instruments. It was like looking at a fairy tale.

The day he met the minister's wife, the gringo was asleep in his hotel room. She talked to Don Arturo like a woman on vacation, and Latins have the driver for the screw of metaphor. They made love on the beach that very night; like two animals they made a hole in the sand. He said she was wet like an orange.

He decided it would be a good idea to go the States with the minister and his wife. The minister met him and thought he was charming. They got on a boat, all three, and watched the lights of Habana get eaten by the ocean as the boat moved along to New York. He got his own private room on the ship, and since the food was part of the service he kept it coming. He got stuffed like a bedbug in a hotel.

After midnight the minister's wife would knock on his door. She sliced in like a sheet of paper and told him her husband had fallen asleep with the Bible on his face. He started talking to her in Spanish, which she half understood, but the warmer she got the more she comprehended. They took advantage of the boat's natural sway. She left for her husband's room before daybreak. Her husband commented over breakfast that the food was better on the boat than in Cuba. Arturo said that better than the food was the soul of Christ.

The boat blew its horns when the lights of New York appeared on the horizon. Arturo looked at it and thought it was a stage in a cabaret getting ready for the night show. It was summertime, and the weather was warm like in Cuba. Some people from the church were on land waiting for the ministerial couple, which now included Don Arturo and his wicker suitcase.

They drove to a small apartment building that was attached to the minister's church on the Lower West Side of Manhattan. They gave Arturo his own room and keys and he went up to take a nap; he dreamt about boats coming out of fruits and whales that became guitars and Siboney Indians hanging dead from rosary beads. They knocked on his door to see if he wanted dinner. He went down to join them, the beef stew was orbiting the Bibles.

The minister and his wife sat next to each other as they introduced Arturo to the other people present, three women and two men who were members of the traveling band. The minister spoke of the purpose of Arturo, his fine guitar playing, and where he could fit in. One of the women informed them all that they would rehearse the following day. The food became invisible like the Holy Spirit.

After dinner Arturo excused himself and said he wanted to go out and look at buildings. To him it was another world, something out of a picture. At first he walked as if the street would cave in under him; he looked at the structures and then went up to them and touched them. He made his way to West 14th Street where he began to see Spanish-speaking people and Argentinean and Spanish restaurants featuring seafood.

118

He saw a Catholic church that was old looking and reminded him of the ones he had seen in pictures of Mexico. When he got close he saw that it was called La Virgen de Guadalupe and was truly fashioned like the Spanish churches of old Mexico. He entered and blessed himself with the cool water that was at the entrance.

After contemplation he marched out into the hot sun. He entered a restaurant and sat down to order coffee. He noticed that the Argentinean waiter spoke a different Spanish than his; it was as if the man hissed at the end of his words. A young woman sat at a table next to him and he started chirping to her like a bird. She joined him and opened up like a fan from Granada.

She told him her father was a merchant seaman stationed in New York. She had come to live with him when her mother passed away in Buenos Aires a couple of years back. She told him that the Lower West Side was an area where Spaniards and Latin Americans were settling. They talked through two cups of coffee. Finally she invited him to her place and he said yes four times.

The apartment was a railroad flat which she shared with her father, who was at the moment out at sea. It was handsomely fixed up with furniture and gadgets from around the world. A picture which had dried butterflies from Brazil hung on one of the walls. A new Iranian rug was on the floor.

Arturo got taken by her beauty and forgot all about the minister and his wife. He played with her eyes and she smiled from the interior. He asked if he could touch her tongue and she shot it out like a cash register drawer. He squeezed it and asked if she had come from Venus. She said that she had arrived from there that very day. This drove him crazy and he went for her buttons.

Arturo got glimpses of the minister and his wife waiting for him and wondering how he was making out in the big metropolis. He thought of what he should do: should he stay the night with the sweet Argentinean rose or track through the dark streets? They fell onto the rug tied together with arms and legs and rolled from one side of the parlor to the other. He fell asleep, his face on her neck. They awoke and chatted. Well, he had to get back. He explained the whole church situation. He left after they arranged to meet the next day at the same restaurant for lunch.

She was golden heaven, and his mind heard trumpets. Angels played harps as he walked back, retracing his path. He found the church and with his own keys entered and went up to his room. He fell onto his bed like a piece of lumber. It is this way that Don Arturo had his first full day in the U.S.A.

With the minister's traveling band he went in and out of cities and towns saving souls. The Depression was on the horizon. Meat had to stretch like rubber bands.

Arturo was an expert at survival. He got tired of plucking wire for the Christian band and massaging the minister's wife. Soon he found his own furnished room in what is now Spanish Harlem; the neighborhood was populated by Germans, Spaniards, and Cubans. On 3rd Avenue there were cigar-making chops (Chin-Chals). He knew Mr. Bustelo when he was getting his coffee beans together. He knew the Valencia family when they had plans to spread their sweetness as the biggest Latin bakery of wedding and specialty cakes in New York City.

When the market crashed he became a street musician, taking a position outside Macy's and sometimes Gimbel's. He played many instruments at the same time, even putting a tambourine on his feet. He sang popular Latin American songs and told jokes. Sometimes he got arrested and he put puppet shows on in the courtroom. The court clerks rolled on the floor.

The manager of Macy's toy department took a liking to his entertainment qualities and hired him to sell puppets and give floor shows inside. Winters came over him like layers of blankets. His hair started to get like pepper that was sprinkled with salt.

As a street musician he began performing in a spot in Greenwich Village. Tired of commuting downtown he moved to the Lower East Side.

Now 78, he still cultivates his famous corner in the Village come spring and summer. He savors memory like espresso coffee. He calls up his beautiful moments with women like an encyclopedia, though his memory sometimes scatters. The details he gives shine like light bulbs and make bridges with each other.

Together we sit and talk, staring at the abandoned buildings on 10th Street where inside doors are still intact and the hinges are lonely for motion. We review time and its fibers. Sipping on white German wine, we both chuckle at life's contradictions. Always spice it with laughter. Remember too much insisting can break even iron. The lights of the building go off and we light two candles and sip in the darkness. His hair shines like white threads of silk.

Don Arturo recognizes the old refrain: All of life is a hole. How so? The man enters the woman's vagina, which can be described as a hole; the infant, you come out of this very hole; you eat food through the hole of your mouth; you breathe through the holes of your nose; you shit through that famous hole; and when you die they drop the total you into a hole in the ground. So you see, all of life is a holy hole. Bet hard on that.

The wine which is sweet and old comes out of the hole located at the top of the bottle. We laugh ourselves through the linoleum, me and Don Arturo, who is 78 and to this day has never been on an airplane. The way he got here the story you have been told.

Old San Juan

Old San Juan looks like a ring worn by an Andaluz sailing on the *Niña* with Columbus. Like a crown of jewels sticking out of the ocean. Spanish Colonial homes look like silk skirts or colorful dresses belonging to belly dancers. With the heat of the sun which comes out without mercy the architecture melts colors as the buildings jump flamenco. Old and full of song, fans like Granada peacocks, Spanish bouquet of flowers, soap Maja, bracelets and Columbian gold, black stone of Congo head, jewelers' windows, Gothic stage. Gypsy song and sailors' narratives of the imagination in long journeys, a storm, a shark, finally entering a bay of turquoise, lifting the anchors notice red coral like worms attached. Boat horns amuse the air as they are blown in the distance and heard everywhere.

One day I was feeding the pigeons in El Parque de las Palomas; they are accustomed to people after generations of proper treatment and fly all over you after their food. A short walk away is a small plaza which looks out towards the ocean. Sitting there my head got light like a pigeon's feather. Looking closely at the edge where the water meets the land, I noticed that the island was in fact moving. Has the land removed itself from its plates? I ask myself like a fool. I look around and penetrate the normality, not even half a second has passed. Am I the first one to make this discovery? Looking deeper I noticed white foam beginning to form and I am sure this thing is moving. I wonder if I should run down the street and start warning people, but what would the people eating bread and drinking coffee say? The men playing dominoes near a Catholic shrine, they'd say after looking at me with eyes of you-know-what, I've seen you before, you must be the one that went down coming up again. It was no doubt we were out. Run! I yell at them. What is this guy? a white hat asks. Because the earth is moving. Now you notice. This is the earth you know, string of cities merging into metropolitan area, outer crust of small towns alight with radio music, do you not know yet the rhythm that is coming? Here we are in the middle of a crisis and the domino players want to get philosophical: What's wrong with you, creature, you threw yourself into the ocean and became a fish? Here you come with that look in your face, that's what happens when you adjust the eyes. Faces are things to read like letters in a word—read what is happening to you even if the dimensions are the sea and sky. Your face is in the pockets made of mirror, your mouth has not opened and yet it is being filled.

Maybe the water is drinking the earth. Is the eye focusing right. A loud noise is heard in the vicinity, a snake is coming out of the horizon, from the balconies beings po-pop and giraffe-neck into what was materializing in the yonder as they sensate an increase in the velocity of the wind. The excuse is no longer coffee and bread, and dominoes no longer count. A serious breeze came in from somewhere and shaved every living thing to its shape. To me the whole thing was not in my head yet; I was still thinking in terms of streets or even towns, the immensity of a whole island moving had no way of being understood. Have you heard any reports on the radio? Things are never settled here and now, there is a kind of solution, endless drift, uncertainty of position. Spanish or English or North American or Hispanic American took on new meanings; those debates which are never settled are now dressed in a new reality. The land has made like the mind, it has finally joined the confusion. It is like the mind, a face once said, broken in half, that's what makes for the misplacement of things from their place in order.

The wind becomes cooler and the radio reports the National Guard has been ordered out. Between San Juan and Mayagüez many people are still asleep who knows in what panoramic light. Some are leaning against doorways comparing the fine points of rooster fighting. Soon the discussions will change, and whatever is happening and wherever heaven is, this whole place is closer to the truth.

I compare green tree edges with the boundaries of the clouds so as to know the velocity at which we are traveling. A soft whistle comes out of the wind. Everything is reviving back to its frequency, the shops are full, the beauty parlors are doing their twists, bicycles appear from side streets, people get clean in their habitual crates, on their mountain slopes, they string their eyes on the vecinic frame in a daze which is being sawn by the birds. Young girls fidget through their drawers to fit themselves into the day, they decorate sculpture, curves in symmetry. Oranges roam the streets with explosive sweetness. Eyes look out onto the ocean where twilight has formed out of its usual material. 400 miles from the equator warm air sugar get head loose like ripeness, body float with pores made of balloons, or have we changed our latitude. I perceive motion towards where I do not know, now we are going since we never thought of it before.

The men who played dominoes near the Catholic shapes saw that even while they laughed at my apparent ignorance, I was already in a better position than they in relationship to an incoming twenty-foot wave that was wetting the tops of the colonial homes so full of history.

The United States was interested in the position of the Puerto Rican people, their whereabouts. Teams of geologists were en route with the Navy. The newsmen on television blossomed with new vocabulary, words like *sima substrata* were making sense. They were interviewing the scientists who said it was that the supporting plates were crisscrossed by the tunnels of caves. Other mechanics were looking for leaks and on a mule was Dr. Sonsabitch from Columbia University, going towards the interior central mountains to see if the foundation of the island was quicksand. If the thing is built on quicksand, who's gonna pay taxes to live in nervous beauty, to be reposed on a verb. Forests are made by the tips of tongues. Many have not been able to sustain the timbre and write letters from afar, as postage rates fluctuate. In Washington, D.C. the government changes the management of Puerto Rico from the Department of War to the Bureau of Missing Persons. That's right, the total and full dislocation. I don't put too much on the wind factor — it writes its epics under the name of Hurakán and comes in its season. There is no preparation, no proper study of history that would have explained this phenomena. This is unprecedented, like when the word *Commonwealth* was first introduced, a what, what is that, there is no direct translation into the Spanish. Here in what's happening, it is now the opposite, the uncommon poverty. The argument of the Popular Democratic Party that we live in a free associated state is now right on the money. Now free to associate, the states change like states of mind and continuously changing every mile. Those who clamored for independence as a political ideal now have its physical counterpart — we are as independent as the fish. All we have to do now is watch out for big mouths.

An island 110 miles long and 36 miles wide is adrift, there is an international emergency, the whole planet is aware of our embarkment. If once we tried to put nails into the ground to become a place unique, to have relations with the minerals and the creatures, to have sovereignty over diplomacy and trade, to exchange fruit for iron, songs for clothing, the hammer of destiny hit the nails from the bottom up and out they came, turning us into a surf board en route to Polynesia with 3.3 million faces, necks and lips.

The United States Navy and Puerto Rican fishermen are trying to get control of this real estate chunk, tugboats are attempting to attach themselves to the sides, they are all going to be pulling in different directions. If it sweeps up near Cuba, grave political problems will burst. Puerto Rico can go alongside another country and make it bigger and in a few generations admire its disappearance, learn to dance differently and put foreign land in its mouth. If it drifted into Haiti or Brazil, we'd have to explain the unexplainable in another land which is another language, and after the exchange of the simplest hellos all we could do is point towards the ocean and come out with a speech like this: We were people living somewhere in the Caribbean, something happened, the land came off its hinges, we are Puerto Ricans. We are somewhere in Puerto Rico but Puerto Rico is somewhere else – in Puerto Rico out of it, it's hard to explain, confusing even if it is explained, and if it is explained it is not comprehended. Who belongs on this boat and where is this boat going?

The domino players soon got a good glimpse of what was rolling; I felt the wind produced by their bodies rushing by me and also heard a guttural sound emerging from their fleeting throats. It was only the wave that was created by the splash of the island going onto its belly, to make the first country that became a floating mass, that became mobile, that took off from its position on the globe. The people on the coast had the best view of the event; they were shocked the most for they could clearly see things moving as in a movie. As if Old San Juan was an old man squatting on the ground who suddenly lifted himself up and took a leap. Wow! like what is the gasoline. If it's not something going, it's something coming. El Morro, the tremendo Spanish fortress, was the scene of many battles with invaders. They came from all sides. It was here that the Dutch pirates were fought off in 1621, the Dutch wanting to take the island and then take the next dot on the Caribbean; it would have been like dominoes falling and Heineken would have been a lot cheaper, and about that cheese they'd have to import mountains of gouda, the crackers we have here. Because we are a flute and the East Trade Winds the musician, the change of position now is a change of melody—keep aware that what you are hearing is air molested by wind. He that holds you and takes must give you something back, it is the order of things, otherwise language would not have made it through the clouds. If the domino players are convinced that it is time to run, it's time to do it without thinking.

We ran enough to keep from drowning but the lips of the wave washed our feet as if we were on the sand by the ocean, it then retreated back to its source and the island was 100 percent ship ahoy. Everything got perfect and went back to itself. The residents, some confused before as to where they were at, are now not confused as to where they are not. I spoke to the domino players while we were drying off our shoes and watching San Juan come back to life. San Juanitis was dancing again, charming again, sitting and flirting like a 19 year-old Spanish rose. One of the domino players kept saying that he had the winning piece in his hand, that he was gonna close the game. It was the double nothing which is called La Chucha which is associated with the State of Virginia. Just a reference beyond its numerical value, a vast emptiness in your hands with two halfs, it means the end or the beginning of the world. He still had it in his hand.

An old painter came out of a doorway and said he had been painting a river within a picture and when he saw the water enter under the door he knew he had synchronized with the element—for good or for bad, he wasn't that celebro about it, just a turn and an outward rush through an open door. Everything that had water in it left with water, even if you thought you were an avocado you would have rushed into the watercress of memory.

I walk back to the public car depot, the fares have remained the same, among the people there are some chuckles about getting wet. Faces look at faces in the cans loaded with passengers, one mouth says to another mouth: Someone is gonna make money off this—if we go north we'd have to start importing coats as the climate gets cold. Conversation flared up as it always does, it being impossible to sit next to someone without talking, without saying or asking, a salutation, this is not New York. And all flights to the city have been canceled; not being able to determine a distance, they can't set a fare. Going towards the village-towns, the jitney van moving within moving, and we look at ourselves with a kind of shit that says as long as we are okay, doing a good speed and in good weather with plenty of tobacco and chicken, with plenty of parcha and transistor radio sets, we can't think too much about what's out there. We might end up in Antarctica or head North towards the States, end up in some place of no illusions like Buffalo, New York, the trees will turn to steel pipes, the eerieness of Lake Erie will supply the wind with hatchets.

Thanks it is to God that no one was killed or injured, not knowing if it is a disaster or nature moving toward its best, listening to each of the opinions of the riders, hearing their mufflers throw out smoke, the familiar trees running by. Now that we are nowhere, we have a better sense of what somewhere could be like. The domino players look at me and remember that I was the one who broke the news to them – they thought I was crazy, saying stupid things like a gringo – they were white-haired old men neatly positioned at their game in the little plaza of San José Church. I told them the truth and ran, now they say they heard my anatomy crack as I positioned to smoke over the horizon. The one with the choocha, he said that it wasn't long after I cleared that he got flashes from the edge of sight. The iris, a lot smarter than what it looks at, knew better and detected a slight flare from the light of the morning sun.

Dominoes on the table, lizards on the window. Light comes in through the feet, a head turns to listen to a report about a floating island going towards a destiny no one knows. Something will occur, forces will jump into the architecture, spilling juice over the columns that hold things up. As the world continues to fold up, we can step on available rock. The dirt eternally changes face, humanity jumps from feature to feature. Because of this situation the mapmakers will never complete their work and all existing maps of the world are inaccurate. What is the cause of this geological mess – it must've been the tunnels of the caves, holes throughout the whole island; the wind blew and they vibrated at the bottom. The earth danced loose with vibratory wind, a saxophonic solo, some kind of hot vapor mixed with minerals. What made it tilt? Horses rumbling through mountains, circling the rim. Trumpet players in search of Shango, the dancers push the ground in with every shuffle. The island took off its hat and flung it at some lover. At some love.

I went into the city like an ignorant country fellow, in search of just the visual excitement, the distances between things, to look at and compare the manner of dress, to see the way women walked. Labyrinths stretching full of chance and surprise. Rush of skeletons in endless flight. Playing with the birds, the ocean is mentioned to me, and walking to the border which has no beginning and no end,I saw the paste of the earth unglue, the knees of nature buckle.

There are many who still do not believe that we are gone, that unless we anchor onto something we will eternally be leaving one place for the other. When you say you're over here you are gonna be over there. Migration is the steady song of being, idea and song looking for food in the wilderness of space. A party mood enters the population like it was Christmas, people have fireworks in the eyeballs. Electricity was coming in and the moon was coming in, green lime floats in rum.

The reports are saying that we are sailing toward Buenos Aires, all the radio stations are blasting tangos, the popular song of Argentina. They played all the ones by Carlos Gardel, the Frenchman who in Buenos Aires was the main exponent. He sang about slum neighborhoods and honor and the surprises of love. The mood of eerieness transformed to a festive atmosphere, sweet syrup pours over the wounds of separation, a pink tissue blankets the confusion.

Back in the village, life intertwined through the bodies who merged with the lies of stability and walked through their days like their yesterdays. I went over to Temple Cafetin in search of my friends. Checo the owner looked indifferent to what was happening, a kind of so-what stare as he mixed drinks over a newspaper which had the whole story on the front page. It said: ROOTLESS ISLAND, had commentaries on the possible whys but not much beyond the observation that it happened. What else could be said of this natural manifestation? Old women light candles to their God. Round and round she goes, where she stops nobody knows. Checo lit a cigar, he told me everything is hot and cool at the same time. The clubs are full, the bars are gay. He served rum with anisette and made one for himself, salud, no matter where we are, we are standing and having this shot of rum. Politically, Checo always wanted one thing or the other. He used to say Either we become a state or we become independent, this Commonwealth lingo makes no sense, hanging like this. It's a nowhere kind of stance, it's not a stance at all, you just stand there while designs are being made around your head. Or this or the other thing and it has got to be a thing of right now. I don't blame the earth, the beauty to get tired and go away. He mixed two more drinks to the music, Palo Viejo playing drums. From the Temple we look towards the street and watch the population, happy and joking and taking things as from a distance, knowing that everything is in the hands of God. The National Guard was all around teaching people the points in a national rescue plan, lifeboats were distributed, helicopters flew overhead. For the time being it was smooth sailing, the sun bouncing against the ground.

It was a Friday, which is always a holiday here called Viernes Social, or have we crossed some kind of international date line and wandered back towards Thursday or jumped over into Saturday? What happens with calendars, not to say anything about time which is to no avail—clocks would have to run faster and go fast forward or get on reverse and fly back. As we move along we will see the shades of motion, compartments in the sky. Everyone keeps their wristwatches for luxury, for mere delight, life is for comfort and for pleasure of the eyes. The radio no longer gives the time of day, it only tells you if the day is light or dark, or shades like twilight. Time is divided into the parts of space, moments are not nailed one after the other, everything is done within an approximation. I'll see you some time in the twilight. Geography is the great subject of all the schools—if we are small, if we are big, where we are, former Caribbean island perhaps floating towards Massachusetts. How can anything get done in proper time, in civic time, a clear place sitting on the second hand of a watch. The publishers of schedules and almanacs are calling for meetings to invent a new system of coding the passage of space through the fibers of the mind in a place that doesn't matter where you are but when you are.

Faces kept coming into the Temple with some kind of force in the cheeks. Checo—blossomed and moved through his bar like Houdini. The more adventure, the more money for me, the more drinks I sell, in the while I smile we are somewhere else, lucky I don't charge you for the benefit of light bulbs. The foreign beer is going up immediately, it has higher transportation tariff now that we are farther from or nearer to one place or the other. The biggest pleasure yacht in the world goes along, may not be far from your neighborhood. From the homes the smell of fish, bacalao serenade, TV dinners, pernil and sweet plantain. It's a carnival out there, Don Stylus reports as he hangs a left into the

Temple. He came down to take the temperature of irregularity, his artisan hands making wooden sculpture, creating statues with sabrette, with measurement, with such fine lines, well-defined scratches, the leg of an ant is heard as it walks from one line to the next. Let your eyes grab, while your hands talk, look at your hands, there is nothing weirder than this, the palm of your hand, the palm where the coconut hangs. Don Stylus wants a Dutch beer, he walks over to the jukebox and drops a nickel into it. A record came on called "Yucca in the Casserole." Hands became nervous with rhythm. Song starts to cook rice while sermon crisscrosses sermon. There is a murmur in the street. We must look like a green woman floating in a turquoise mirror. Don Stylus tightened all the heads with ribbons. He snaps, no matter where this place goes I'm gonna find stone to chisel, wood to cut, gold to mold, something to use my pliers on, for my hammer to give life to something beautiful out of a scrap given up as useless, something out of coral and potent, pretty and useful like a cane with snakes and palm huts carved into it, a swan grilled onto a mirror. Life is running away, the positions of the stars are changing, music folds from guitars to drums, lyrics swing from the flower of a new love to betrayal and disillusionment. Checo is gathered into his guayabera shirt, he looks at Don Stylus and discovers that the man is asleep. He signals for my attention and points out the circumstances. Well, I'll have a beer on him, I say. Let's wake him up, says a loose patron. Hey, Don Stylus jumps up as if a small hurricane came out of him. Someone tell me what's happening, I am seasick, where am I. The day gathered inside of him till he was a person. He ran out into the breeze, he heard the helicopters and was told the news, asleep or awake it doesn't make any sense, it was safer while he was dreaming. Nothing is wrong, just that we are not attached to the earth, that we are moving. Quality of air is constant trance. The horns of a boat coming to port are heard, they sound celestial in the morning sun of the mountainous region where trees dream with flying reptiles. A forest arrives into a house and enters the slices of the animals.

I run south or north or is it west or did I run east to catch up with Don Stylus and tell him about Old San Juan. How I went as always to see the motion of sugar and salt, to have the birds in Parque de las Palomas tell me their dreams. It was in one of these conferences that they told me to watch the edges, and walking to the beginning of the land I detected the movement and popped to where a group of lizards were playing dominoes and told them what was up. They told me Go home and sleep, you country boy, mountaineer, go walk your cow. Don Stylus looked back at me and everything around us disappeared, all the green and red, all the sounds and rattles. He understood and that was what was important.

Where is this caravel going? What will the documents of history manifest? Which radars will pick us up as we sail through all available water? Pigeons run the city of San Juan, they are free to do as they wish. From the hidden balconies of fear there is this hope tight like a knot around the neck that longs to manifest a peaceful home to sleep in, a secure ground for the flavors of the soul. Tomorrow we all may become ice or achieve our truthful heat. All aboard this enchanted traveling garden, it is nighttime and three million birds are asleep. Dreaming.

Some Thoughts as We Approach the 500th Anniversary of the Discovery of the Americas

Puerto Rico: an isle in the Caribbean where I was born in a wooden house which is now a popular cafetin (a small combination bar and grocery store) with a loud jukebox featuring the bolero music of Felipe Rodriguez, Trio Los Panchos and more Salsa than you can throw on fish. Ruled by Spain for 400 years, we became a possession of the United States as a result of the Spanish-American War. Goddamn Spaniards lost, tyrants that they were with our indigenous population.

Understanding that the history of this small planet is migration and expansion as one group of people with their culture and language move in on another. It makes me wonder about Spain and how unprepared they were for expansion in 1492. It was the same year that they were fighting the Arabs in Granada to regain Castilian territory. It was one of Europe's most divided nations, a land conquered and reconquered. It had no linguistic unity to speak of. Within its borders people spoke Basque, Catalan, Castilian, Aragonese, Hebrew, Arabic, and then there were the Gypsies with their universal speech stew. I must then believe in a sacred motion of history, a hidden power moving the strings of events. Regardless of all of those obstacles, off they went, and their thirst was such that they made it all the way to Guam and the Philippines.

Who were the deckhands sailing on the first trips? Could they have been Moors and Jews who had to vacate anyway—after all, it was the Spanish Inquisition that was coming, and those priests would not even forgive their own mothers. Life aboard the caravels must've been mind-exploding. It is well documented that Spanish authorities emptied many prisons and gave the prisoners an offer they couldn't refuse. Either you go off with this Genovese racketeer to wherever or you stay in that cell. Try and picture life within a medieval Spanish prison. To be booked upon a sailing circus, even if it was going to hell, was indeed a blessing. On board it was a great bazaar. Some of the men were speaking Spanish, Columbus was speaking Italian, others were yapping in Arabic, another group was spouting Ladino.

The Spanish language had been freshly hatched out of a Latin chicken. Here they come, three boats on the horizon. Swarthy bearded men singing coplas and smoking hashish, playing Arabian la'uds or the emerging Spanish guiter. With such a band how could they not get lost. The myth of the earth being flat was for popular consumption. Columbus knew he was going somewhere. Had he not read Plato, who knew that there was a bright sun shining upon a garden in the West. Had not Marco Polo been up earlier taking a stroll; he should have detected a curvature upon the earth's crust on such a long venture. All of that because his palate was unsatisfied with the local cuisine. It's a long way to go for the gourmet section of a supermarket. He found the spaghetti, Columbus found the tomato sauce. The Spaniards also ran into chile which must've awakened the Andalusian gift of blasphemy, they are the world's greatest cursers. We could pretend that the real reason for the Spanish voyages of exploration was an unconscious urge for guayaba; but lo and behold, their mouths were not as opened as Marco Polo's. When a group of Tainos (Caribbean natives) bestowed some juicy pineapples upon their unexpected visitors, they immediately went into facial contortions, running into the bushes to vomit. It was one of the first encounters of the native fruit with the Iberian tongue. That alone should have been adequate warning of the massacres to come.

The colonization proceeded on a massive scale. The island of Santo Domingo saw one of the first cities of the Spaniards go up. Its principle street was named Calle de las Damas. Old San Juan came up after; in the chambers of El Morro, the old Spanish fortress built to protect the city from coastal invasion, one can still hear the cries of the Tainos jailed and slaughtered within. After 1500 the main thrust of Spanish colonization went towards Mexico City. It was in Mexico were the Spanish language was hindered the most, it had to confront the Mayan and Aztec tongues, which were rich and abundant. Unlike in the Caribbean, the native populations of Mexico and other parts of Central and South America were not extinguished. The battle and fusion in the Antilles was between the African and Spanish, with the indigenous population disappearing but still leaving a strong racial and cultural influence, making us Caribbeans the true harmonizers of world civilizations, the true Raza Cósmica that Mexican educator José Vasconcelos wrote about.

133

In Puerto Rico the gold was emptied from the rivers by the newcomers, who gave it a value much more than its symbolism for the sun. Occasionally I venture out on the edges of El Río Mula, close to my Aguas Buenas home, hoping that perhaps they missed a nugget or two.

As we approach the 500th anniversary of the discovery of the Americas by Columbus, Puerto Rico still remains in a colonial situation, controlled economically and militarily by the U.S. but not culturally or spiritually. After over 90 years of U.S. presence we remain speakers of Spanish, a culture rich in folkloric traditions of song, music and dance. We have also witnessed the U.S. invasion of Panama as 23,000 men were sent to capture a single individual. It could be a sign that the Good Neighbor Policy of the past is coming back in style for the nineties. If you have any doubts about the colonial status of Puerto Rico, just note that 18 days after Hurricane Hugo brushed through our island, President Bush sent Dan Quayle's wife to inspect the damage, which she did within two and a half hours. Her visit to the island was managed in such a way that the governor of the island, Hernández Colón, was notified two hours before her plane was to arrive. When the first lady of Puerto Rico, the governor's wife, rushed out to the airport to greet the visitor, she was informed by a spokeswoman for Mrs. Quayle that the vice president's wife would not ride in the same limousine with her into San Juan. Proud Puerto Rican lady that she is, she left faster than a lizard's head can pop.

If plans to invade Panama were at hand for over six months, as U.S. media indicates, there was some consideration for the Sugar Ray/Roberto Duran fight. Think of all the millions that would have been lost internationally if the U.S. Marines had invaded three days before the fight. No, capitalism knows better, the fight must go on.

Spain had its golden period during the Arabian occupation, which commenced in A.D. 711 and lasted some 800 years. The Arabs encouraged the study of science and the development of the arts. Public libraries were established in the large cities. Religious tolerance allowed Jews as well as Christians to practice their manner of worship and to communicate one with the other. Men of learning such as Averroës, Avicenna, ibn 'Arabi began to translate and comment upon dormant Greek classics, contributing to the reawakening of Europe. It was a place of great architecture, great centers of medicine and beautiful paths that led to gardens where fountains were flowing with water.

The Moors gave the Visigoths much to improve and enhance their civilization. There was much intermarriage and many Christians abandoned their religion for that of their conquerors.

It is clear and recognizable that much of what came upon those boats from Spain across the Atlantic contained this Islamic Dynamism. The Spanish is full of Arabian words as well as indigenous words; add to that the inclusion of Africa to our world and you get a picture of the rich universal vocabulary that we are coming down the mountains and streets with. As a Hispanic of the Americas I look back upon our history of turbulence, of conquests and migrations. The extinction of the indigenous peoples of the Caribbean is one of mankind's great tragedies. Despite this anthropological knowledge, there are moments in my hometown of Aguas Buenas when the sentiment and appearance of the Tainos swell all of my senses and the small streets of my childhood become ageless.

It is difficult to conceive of Spain as merely a European country, especially its southern region, Andalusia (Al Andaluz), rich in Moorish and Gypsy blood. Perhaps a new category is needed, something that would place it between Europe and the East. Spain is the one country in the world where the notorious wandering Gypsies have established traditions of song and dance and have settled into community. The Gypsies and the Moors are the soulful base of the rich musical traditions of Iberia. Puerto Rico inherited one of the great classical musicians and composer of the twentieth century from Spain in the figure of the cellist Pablo Casals, who made this tropical isle his home. He lived and produced great music here and has left an enduring love for classical music in a sizable portion of our population.

Franco (who was not French)—a modern-day arrogant Cortés patriarchal pig do-as-I-say tyrannical nut, the kind we know of very well in Latin America, both in terms of political power and family relations—had his men hunt down and assassinate the country's greatest living poet, Federico García Lorca, during the Spanish Civil War. One of Lorca's biographers points out that the firing squad took off the gold ring and watch which he was wearing but failed to detect a belt buckle of high-quality gold. Since the whereabouts of his grave remain a mystery, I feel that somewhere in Spain there is a golden light emanating out of the earth. The message was clear. Miguel Hernández, another passionately brilliant poet, died in one of Franco's jails. Spanish writers, intellectuals and painters began to abandon their homeland in fear of what was obviously coming.

Once again Spaniards migrated to the Americas. The poet and scholar Pedro Salinas landed on the shores of San Juan and was able to write and continue to develop. He recognized the richness of Puerto Rican Spanish, a language of strong expressiveness full of proverbs and folktales which poured down from the campesino mountains. It is the campesinos who keep particular vernaculars alive and pumping worldwide. Language seems to stagnate in the cities, where it is cut off from agriculture and thus from rhythm; in the cities people sing less. Peasants are nowadays an endangered species being replaced by individuals who are products of the industrial-technological processing age. Ecology-minded radicals should take up their cause, for of what good is it to have a good green earth if a bunch of jerks are going to be the ones to live in it. You can see the human rootlessness in the form of the Yuppies who now fill most large North American cities. Career freaks who opinionate nothing but go out and pay $6.00 for an avocado sandwich. In Puerto Rican terms that is a financial disgrace and enough sin to have the Gods recycle you into the same kind of nerd. Pedro Salinas defended the importance of tradition in life as well as literature, for without it there is no real freedom.

The Nobel Laureate Juan Ramón Jiménez also made Puerto Rico his home for a period of his life. Unlike their ancestors, these men came with their pens and not with their swords. All of them were embraced by the thriving University of Puerto Rico at Río Piedras, where they were all given opportunities to teach and a generation of Puerto Rican students were blessed by their presence.

San Juan of the mid-forties offered a rich cultural life to both exiles and natives. The music and lecture halls were always full. Old San Juan, the second city of the Hispanic Americas, had its art galleries and bohemian cafes, as it still does today, where conversation and creativity soared to great heights as Europe slaughtered itself across the Atlantic.

María Teresa Babin, one of Puerto Rico's prominent poets and educators, had front row seats on the whole drama of Spanish exiles as well as the meaning of the great adventure and experiment that was unleashed at the encounter of Spanish culture with the indigenous civilizations of the so-called New World. She believed strongly upon native

ground: "Somos criollos del Caribe y no españoles; somos puertori-
queños y no otra cosa." María Teresa Babin died in 1989, the same year
that I came back to Puerto Rico. She once told me that "we can't live
in the 19th century," meaning that she knew that the Jíbaro folkloric
culture would have to go through transformations. Teresa Babin will
live in all the centuries to come as each singing bird chirps the letters
of her verses.

Now about this business of the 500th anniversary of the discovery of
the Americas by Columbus (over here it's Colón and it has more pitfalls).
It seems that everybody and their mother has discovered the Americas.
Very true it all is for it is well documented that the Chinese were in
Mexico. Sinaloa for everybody. Central American pre-Colon(ization)
art is abundant in Buddhist symbols and figures of Tibetan priests.
Phoenician and Egyptian hieroglyphs have been found in Peru – and I
mean to the letter – and there it is, the thing itself. There's that gigantic
Olmec sculpture with African features. Ah, no that the Vikings. . . that
the . . . the . . . I discovered America in El Guanabano of Aguas Buenas
on a Sunday morning of February 1949 in Colmado-Cafetin El Poema,
where a group of pueblanos make rum evaporate as I walk by and hear
Felipe Rodriguez singing the songs of his memories.

The truth of the matter is that only artists discover for they discover
things that are not of this world.

The Popular Muse Belongs to Everybody

I went to El Colmado to get a plantain when I saw that she was there with her husband. I'd always see her in the distance with her married status, the beam of her eyes stronger than Radio Voz, broadcasting to the nerves of a sensitive insect. It was the closest I'd ever come within view of her eyes, it was like a nuclear meltdown, focusing upon them made me nervous and I dropped a plantain back into the wooden box where they were stationed. I saluted her husband, who is an appreciable fellow known for the composition of his verses in the town. He is a popular poet, he has an established style and stays within a certain frame. I was going to use the phrase "limited vocabulary range" but that narrow pen can only be seen from the audience, he himself is fulfilled after each poem is accomplished. The lyrics of songs are the neighbors of his poems. He himself recites them out loud. He is one of the oral-popular poets. They are like one guitar string down from the singers. Oral poets expend themselves within declaim, and there is a distinction between oral and popular poets. The oral poets have memories like the ocean, they recall poems and belt them out precisely word for word, the poems become part of their body through the gestures they make. The poem may contain enough passion for them to drop down to their knees, squeezing tears out of a spellbound audience. Popular poets don't, as a law, recite their poems out loud, they compose them in the privacy of their lives.

I had an uncle who was a popular poet who wrote many of his verses upon brown paper bags and sometimes upon cardboard. Popular poets are locked within a frame, they are stuck on a dime's worth of themes, and from there they do not venture out into deeper jungle. Love and betrayal, religious devotion, the beauty of the landscape, poems about mothers, sometimes nationalism: they churn within that circle. Their poems are person-to-person, they work out action that adds up to tragedy, movements that are boats upon the rivers of sentiment, observed sadness that comes to a boil within predictable relations. Their ideas are released from the lips of history, the speeches of others, usually the elders of their own family, someone that fascinated them as children. Perhaps they lived up on a wooden house and a certain campesino would visit them every Sunday around 3 o'clock to drink coffee with the family. This campesino's voice would resound through the wooden house, vibrate through the lumber and nails of its creation, above and below chirping birds, within a background of roosters and scattering chickens. He would speak proclaimative, as if he were talking to the public in general, declaring himself with a tone as if he were addressing a court in Sevilla, as if he were begging Saint Peter to let him into heaven. What he was talking about was probably half nothing, recounting something trivial out of everyday existence, he had a manner of enlarging events, making the smallest affairs into mountains. In an agricultural region where time moves like the growth of plants, any event would make the lips of talkers. The young poet's ears were like caves listening—once he heard the campesino retell a story that years later he would recount within a poem, the campesino was retelling it for the millionth time, the story about a certain Jíbaro named Don Monson who lived up upon the highest peak, the cima of a mountain. It is said that one day he ventured upon his horse into town, tied his horse next to a cantina and took a walk to observe the progress, when a certain petty town official called out to him and referred to him as "un individuo," not knowing what the word *individuo* meant. Don Monson took offense. Who is an individual, perhaps it is the very mother that bore you, he shot back. No one calls me an individual, this matter is not gonna stop here. Stay like this, wait a minute: I'm going back up and will come back down with a sabre. No one, no one, not even a town official calls Don Monson an individual. The storyteller takes a sip of coffee and stirs it with a spoon 'cause the host had told him to shake it around 'cause the sugar was at the bottom. He went on to say that Don Monson came back down and chased the town official over a mountain and across a river. The family would laugh towards jaw cracking as they saw the pictures of a movie. That country person swallowing what he considered an insult, that singular machete of honor shining in the darkness of his mind like the appearance of a virgin between the dark night of two trees.

Those are the occasions that become occurrences inside the verses of the popular, they come out of the mountains and the streets, they are mathematicians adding and subtracting the figures of drama, the exchanges of men and women who hurry through the circus of life within the fixed cabinets of verses that always rhyme, written in décimas or coplas, arranged like flowers for an occasion. The poets obey a formula of charm which they have acquired through custom. They are the ones who compose eulogies and accompany funerals to the tombstone, they write poems in praise of the visible qualities of a given life leaving the little music hidden inside for the angels to decipher. The style and the syntax is like the pillars of a Catholic church. Popular poetry is not direct common speech, it has air to it, the words are paved with the fantasy of marble, Italian archways emerging out of green sierras, columns of straw hats singing celestial Latin. That Galician wind that creates the hypocritical terminal lisp, that crown of superiority. The person is never in the poet when he sits down to write, he takes flight to a nation of mist in the sky. The moment, forget about the moment, who wants to write about picking coffee or a swinging machete slicing cane. Half the observation is made and the writer grasps what he can. How pretty it is. Men throwing flowers at passing women in the plaza – that is popular verse. Refrains told by mothers and grandmothers as advice to children in growth. Guessing jingles to make penetrative thought – these are all suspirations that flow within the ether and get ahold of people at random without them reaching, working or doing any more than just being. The rhythm that is around appearing. What drives the insects to kiss and take flight.

Her burning soul boiled the plantains in my hands, her eyes transmitting pictures of a place, her heart drumming the fibers of a time and the shape of an amorous night.

The stock of people that accumulates everyday at El Colmado were in their usual positions by habit. It was I who surprised the content rushing out the door upon potassium radiation, I was called in by a vegetative whistle. Ripening plantains next to the coconuts. Next to aroma the palate has no powers of resistance, a taste which takes a caravel back towards the Ivory Coast of Africa, but even sooner than that a tent is suspended between the continents. Her eyes lean against the moisture of my tongue looking out towards the sea, where the fish who are popular habitat look for the language of my hook.

A Background Note for
"The Popular Muse Belongs To Everybody"

The muse has been turned into powder
Sprinkled into the ocean
It has ventured back out upon the
Tongue of a lizard
To make trees and plazas
And the edge which is where
I fall between the balconies
Yellow dresses adjacent
To lush encounters
Between a thought and hanging
sweetness

At any moment it has no place
Who would own it tries
To imprison the wind
It makes desires that take
Shape
Worth more than Catholic
Churches made of gold

It could be a frog
Or a song
The seams of dresses
The drop of tropical
Land into azul water
The height
The low

It paid rent at the formation
And talks with feet eyes and
Rocks
It could be standing next to you
and nowhere to be seen

I wait with a gourd full
of inspiration
For a chip to fall from
The festival fireworks
To favor me
And set me on fire.

Victor Hernández Cruz was born in Puerto Rico in 1949. His highly acclaimed first book, *Snaps*, was published the year he turned nineteen. His books include *Mainland, Tropicalization, By Lingual Wholes,* and *Rhythm, Content and Flavor.* He has received numerous awards, including a National Endowment for the Arts Fellowship, and a Creative Artists Program Service (CAPS) grant. His legendary dynamic reading ability has led to his being twice crowned as the World Heavyweight Poetry Champion in Taos.